"A very provocative and unusual book aimed at recovering the human significance of philosophical questions and answers. It should be required reading, especially for 'philosophers.'"—John E. Smith, Clark Professor of Philosophy, Yale University.

"Needleman is deeply dissatisfied with the approach to philosophy that only gathers, identifies, and reconstructs ideas and problems. . . . Genuine philosophy, he insists, includes a deeply personal questioning, full of wonder—a passionate seeking (akin to *eros*) for that which is higher and greater than oneself. . . . I admire the direction and purpose of this book, for it counterbalances tendencies to make mere verbiage of philosophy, and it legitimizes personal needs and drives as part of the search for truth."—Walter D. Wagoner, *The Christian Century*

"Needleman is someone who beautifully fulfills Hilaire Belloc's description of a great don or college professor: a scholar for whom the life of learning, teaching, writing, and living is a continuous act. For many, academic inquiry is a narrow field of specialization. For Jacob Needleman, it is a pilgrimage, a search, a journey into the world where he might find and serve others, and find and serve himself."—Kevin Starr, *San Francisco Examiner*

"Needleman has the ability to ask the kind of unexpected, unconventional questions that force one's seeking to a different level, and he is more demanding, sometimes it seems impossibly demanding, of religious thinking and practice than most participants in the various traditions are. He is certainly true to his calling as a philosopher in his conviction that 'the unexamined life is not worth living.' He proves, he wonders, he pushes, he challenges us, and certainly himself, to see if the way we live, what we think and do, is really all we can hope for, aspire to."—*Parabola*

"A deeply moving book. . . . The author is not merely a competent academic scholar and skilled teacher. He is also close to the deep wellsprings that nourish the human spirit, and he leads us to them in his book."—*New Catholic World*

Also by Jacob Needleman

Consciousness and Tradition (1982)

Lost Christianity (1980)

Speaking of My Life (Editor) (1979)

Understanding the New Religions (1978)
(Editor, with George Baker)

On the Way to Self Knowledge (1976)
(Editor, with Dennis Lewis)

A Sense of the Cosmos (1975)

Sacred Tradition and Present Need (1974)
(Editor, with Dennis Lewis)

The Sword of Gnosis (Editor) (1974)

Religion for a New Generation (1973)
(Editor, with A. K. Bierman and James A. Gould)

The New Religions (1970)

Being-in-the-World (1963)

The Heart of Philosophy

THE HEART
OF PHILOSOPHY

by Jacob Needleman

1817

Harper & Row, Publishers, San Francisco
Cambridge, Hagerstown, New York, Philadelphia
London, Mexico City, São Paulo, Singapore, Sydney

Grateful acknowledgment is made to the following for permission to reprint excerpts from previously published material:

Basil Blackwell Publisher: Extracts from *Philosophical Investigations* by Ludwig Wittgenstein. Reprinted by permission of Basil Blackwell Publisher.

J. M. Dent & Sons, Ltd.: Excerpts from *My Confession* by Leo Tolstoy, translated by Leo Wiener. By kind permission of J. M. Dent & Sons Ltd., London.

Hafner Press: Excerpts from *Critique of Judgment* # 23 by Immanuel Kant. Adapted from the translation by J. H. Bernard. Hafner Press, a Division of Macmillan, 1951.

Harper & Row, Publishers, Inc., and Blond & Briggs, Ltd.: Specified excerpts from pp. 51, 52, 54 in *Small is Beautiful* by E. F. Schumacher. Copyright © 1973 by E. F. Schumacher. Reprinted by permission of Harper & Row, Publishers, Inc.

Humanities Press, Inc., and Routledge & Kegan Paul, Ltd.: Excerpts from *Tractatus Logico-Philosophicus* by Ludwig Wittgenstein. Humanities Press Inc., Atlantic Highlands, N.J. 07716, and Routledge & Kegan Paul, Ltd., London.

Oxford University Press: Excerpts from *The Dialogues of Plato*, translated by Benjamin Jowett, 4th ed., 1953. Reprinted by permission of Oxford University Press.

Penguin Books, Ltd.: Excerpts from Plato, *The Symposium*, trans. Walter Hamilton. Penguin Classics, 1951, pp. 100-105, 107, 110-111. Copyright © 1951 by Walter Hamilton. Reprinted by permission of Penguin Books, Ltd.

Random House, Inc.: An excerpt from the *Duino Elegies*, from *The Selected Poetry of Rainer Maria Rilke*, translated by Stephen Mitchell. Copyright © 1982 by Stephen Mitchell.

Library of Congress Cataloging in Publication Data

Needleman, Jacob.
  THE HEART OF PHILOSOPHY.

  1. Philosophy I. Title
B72.N43   1986   101   85-45719
ISBN 0-06-250645-5

87 88 89 90 10 9 8 7 6 5 4 3 2

To the memory of my mother,
Ida Seltzer Needleman

Contents

Preface

In my experience as a reader and writer of books, all prefaces, forewords, and introductions divide naturally and invariably into two categories. One kind expresses the author's sense of strength, hope, and vision; the other more or less honestly manifests the realization of his limitations. The former, written before all the other chapters of the book, are generally lengthy. The latter are written after the book is finished and are usually quite brief. In this they call to mind the story that is told of a certain Scottish minister, a man of great renown and position, who graciously condescended to deliver a sermon in a small rural church run by a struggling young minister who was an admirer of his. The great man proudly ascends the high, spiral staircase leading up to the pulpit and proceeds to speak for an hour or more only to see that, by the time he is finished, half the congregation has walked out and the other half is fast asleep. Crestfallen, he slowly descends the long spiral staircase and meekly asks his younger colleague what he did wrong. The young minister answers him quite simply: "Had you ascended, Sir," he says, "in the way that you descended, then you might have descended in the way that you ascended."

Briefly stated, then, the aim of this book is to show the place that great philosophical ideas can occupy in the everyday life of contemporary men and women. It is my view that the weakening of authentic philosophy in our century has resulted in a form of collective and individual pathology that has far deadlier consequences than is generally imagined. We live in a time of metaphysical repression and this repression must be lifted. The various forms of psychological and sexual repression that modern psychiatry has successfully fought against are as nothing when compared to the stifling of the love of meaning, which phrase actually is the definition of philosophy. The love of meaning, the search for meaning, is the only real, objective force for good in the life of modern man. Everything else we hope for and wish for ourselves and our children depends upon it.

Such is the argument of this book. In Part I, I attempt to show where great ideas come from—why they have so little power in shaping our lives and what is needed to change this situation. In Part II, I try to demonstrate that the love of meaning is the central, organic fact about the structure of human nature, a fact that has been either ignored or misunderstood in our culture. To show this, I turn to children. It is through working with young people that I have become convinced of this fact about human nature, and in this part of the book I attempt to reproduce the essence of my experiences teaching philosophy to adolescents and their parents. In Part III, I try for nothing less than a redefinition of the history of philosophy in the West, inviting, as it were, Descartes, Hume, Kant, and Wittgenstein, among others, into our noblest dreams and deepest yearnings.

Needless to say, with aims such as these, only the briefest of prefaces is permitted.

Acknowledgments

I am deeply grateful to the officers, students, and parents at San Francisco University High School—especially Headmaster Dennis Collins, Louis Knight, and Paul Chapman—for their sensitive support and encouragement of my work at their school. Although the students and parents depicted in this book are fictitious, I have tried to portray the *essence* of what transpired between us as faithfully as possible. I only hope that what they received from the study of philosophy corresponds in some small measure to the richness of my own experience in knowing and working with them.

I am also grateful to the Threshold Foundation Bureau of London for a grant that enabled me to undertake the experiment of teaching philosophy to high-school students.

I wish to thank my colleague and friend, Professor John Glanville of the San Francisco State University Department of Philosophy, for his meticulous reading of portions of this manuscript and for his wise and forthright suggestions. My thanks also to Professor Peter Radcliffe for a conversation that helped me to think my own thoughts about Wittgenstein.

To Olivia Byrne and Regina Eisenberg, who generously and endlessly assist my work in ways too numerous to mention, my heartfelt and continuing thanks. And I am also grateful to Marilyn Felber who not only typed the manuscript with extraordinary care, but who also provided an insightful reading of the contents.

Finally, I wish to express gratitude to and for my editor, Toinette Lippe, for understanding both the book and its author and for doing her remarkable best to improve the former while preserving the latter. And, of course, to Marlene Gabriel, who has transformed the function of literary agent into something warm and wondrous.

PART I

Philosophy, Where Are You?

CHAPTER 1

Introduction

Man cannot live without philosophy. This is not a figure of speech, but a literal fact that will be demonstrated in this book. There is a yearning in the human heart that is nourished only by real philosophy and without this nourishment man dies as surely as if he were deprived of food or air. But this part of the human psyche is not known or honored in our culture. When it does break through to our awareness, it is either ignored or treated as though it were something else. It is given wrong names; it is not cared for; it is crushed. And eventually, it may withdraw altogether, never again to appear. When this happens, man becomes a thing. No matter what he accomplishes or experiences, no matter what happiness he knows or what service he performs, he has in fact lost his real possibility. He is dead.

The fear of this inner death has begun to surface in the modern world. In quiet moments, an individual senses this fear of dying inwardly and sees that all the other fears of his life—his physical and psychological fears—are in no way related to it. At the same time, he senses—along with this fear—a yearning or love unknown to him in his ordinary life. He sees that none of the other loves of his life—his family, his work, perhaps not even his God— are related to that yearning for something he cannot name. And he wonders what he can do to heal this profound division in himself between the wish for being and his psycho-social needs. Neither ordinary religion, nor therapy, nor social action, nor adventure, nor work, nor art can bridge these two fundamental motivations within him. But no sooner does a man move into the activities of his life than the awareness of this division within himself is forgotten.

What will help him remember? For it is absolutely essential that he remember this truth about himself. If he does not, he will be absorbed by the external forces of nature and society. He will be "lived" by the emotions, opinions, obligations, terrors, promises, programs, and conflicts that comprise the day-to-day life of every human being. He will forget that there are actually two separate lives within him and that these disparate lives need to be related to each other. He will strive for happiness, creativity, love, service to the higher; for vitality, commitment, honor; for understanding, health, integrity; for safety, exhilaration, passionate involvement—but nothing of this will be possible for him in the state of metaphysical forgetfulness. As long as he does not remember the real twofold structure of his being, he and the life around him will form themselves into a tissue of illusion.

The function of philosophy in human life is to help man remember. *It has no other task.* And anything that calls itself philosophy which does not serve this function is simply not philosophy.

But modern man has strayed so far from philosophy that he no longer even knows what this sort of remembering is. We think of memory only as mental recall because the experience of deep memory has vanished from our lives. Therefore, I ask you not to turn to the dictionary or to modern psychological texts for clarification about remembering. It is not something that can be defined right at the outset; its meaning will emerge as we proceed—this I promise.

There is something else I must state here at the outset—as a sort of disclaimer, even as a warning. Philosophy is not an answer to anything. Nor, on the other hand, is it merely the technique of asking questions and criticizing assumptions. Philosophy is not clever. It is not cold. It is not angry. Yet it is disturbing, troubling. Moreover, the trouble it brings will never disappear, will never have an end. Why? Because no sooner does a man remember than he immediately forgets. Therefore, over and over again, he must be reminded—and such reminders are not always pleasant.

I began teaching philosophy some twenty years ago. In those days even academic colleagues looked at you a little queerly when you told them your field. To scientists, you were generally regarded as a "metaphysician"—a particularly dirty word to them: someone who worried about matters beyond the realm of any sane, rational verification. To colleagues in the fields of literature or art, on the other hand, you were merely a logic-chopper. At the very best you were feared as an insensitive thinking machine that could confute any point of view, even the most hallowed, just for the sadistic fun of it. As for people outside the academic profession, there matters were even worse. Anyone foolish enough to admit he was a philosopher invited either outright ridicule or else victimization by a cracker-barrel Aristotle who would, free of charge, present you with an endless string of bloated opinions about everything that had appeared in the newspapers, including the Sunday edition and all the supplements, for the past week. Or else, you were simply met with uncomprehending silence. And then there were the occasions when you were mistaken for something else and found yourself listening to someone's marital problems, medical complaints, or even to an improvised religious confession.

Things are different now. In fact, it is nothing short of remarkable to see what the word "philosophy" now evokes in people from all walks of life: businessmen, scientists, psychologists, doctors, artists—even athletes and politicians. Not a trace of ridicule. On the contrary, more often than not the response is a word or a gesture that says, in effect: "Have you found it? Does it really exist? Can you tell it to me?" Here "it" refers to any number of things, all of which may be summed up by the phrase, no longer a cliché, "the meaning and purpose of life." And the cracker-barrel Aristotle has also changed in remarkable ways—if only because the newspapers he depends on continuously report events that all by themselves raise really penetrating philosophical questions.

Open today's newspaper and you will see: Events are becoming "philosophical." To begin with, there is the endless stream of technological innovations transmuting the way human beings conduct their lives and regard reality. Here is a report about the latest developments in computer technology in which we are also informed that the computer is "an extension of human intelligence." Here, news about discoveries in genetic research that will enable us, and therefore tempt us, to make choices that human beings could never before make: about the sex of our children, about the creation of new life forms, about the very structure of our bodies. But, in order to make such choices, what sort of knowledge do we need?—about the larger sense of biological life, for example, or about the real function of the human body in the whole of life. These are matters for philosophy. And this sort of news happens a hundred times over every day throughout our society and throughout our lives: how and what we eat, drink, and breathe; how we suffer illness; how long and in what state of consciousness we live and die; what we wear; how we occupy our spare time and the time of our children; how we make love; how we work and how we conduct our personal relationships. Absolutely every detail of living is now under the direction of this new talmud of technological change. But where are the philosophical commentaries in the margins of this talmud?—that is what people want and need now. Certainly, commentaries abound, offered by sociologists, historians, journalists, physicians, psychiatrists; and certainly almost every magazine and newspaper offers guidance on what used to be called moral questions. However, none of this is exactly to the point; the point is philosophy. The point is: What is reality? What is the purpose of man's life on earth? How ought we to live? What is the difference between good and evil, and why does evil exist?

An Ayatollah Khomeini brings the world toward the brink

of war; Pope John Paul II galvanizes millions of Americans; nine hundred followers of Jim Jones kill themselves in Guyana. The sociology and politics of such events are fascinating; the psychological and economic components are complex and subtle. But behind it all is the question of religion itself, and this question exists in everyone, consciously or not: Does God exist? What is the difference between true religion and false religion? These are matters for philosophy.

It is the same in everything: the energy crisis; the status of women; the influence of television and media; the creaking financial and economic structure of the nations of the world; the population explosion; pollution of the environment; crime; abortion; divorce; drugs. In human civilization, and in the individual life of every human being, behind every problem to be solved, there is a question of philosophy to be asked—and not only asked as we usually ask, but to be pondered and lived with as a reminder of something we have forgotten, something essential. Our culture has generally tended to solve its problems without experiencing its questions. That is our genius as a civilization, but it is also our pathology. Now the pathology is overtaking the genius, and people are beginning to sense this everywhere.

A geophysicist can tell us a great deal about the energy resources of the planet, but he can tell us nothing about man's proper relationship to the earth. A sociologist can tell us about the social patterns of crime, but he can tell us nothing about the real meaning of crime as a twisted aspect of man's longing for freedom. We can hear much from historians and see vivid pictures created by novelists dealing with the failures and the mistaken turnings of human life. But who can tell us why things in general always work out differently in practice than they do in theory?

But wait, we are moving too fast. Already one begins to feel that deadening process setting in which inexorably drains the real life out of philosophy. It is not so simple to name the questions of philosophy. These questions, the questions of real philosophy, have a certain quality we must pay great attention to, a quality we must identify and care for. These questions must touch the heart. As a general rule, the great questions of philosophy are those that we have all but given up hope of ever seeing asked or answered, questions that somewhere deep within us, in the child within us, we long to think about, dream about. These are questions that have a certain quality of magic about them. That means they touch something in us, something that is at the same time utterly intimate and impersonal, something that we can refer to by the paradoxical words "the warmth of real objectivity."

Like any trained professor of philosophy, I can reel off a list of the classical and conventional "problems of philosophy": the "mind-body problem" (how can mind, which is immaterial, act upon the body, which is material?); the "problem of universals" (do general entities, such as "goodness" or "mankind," really exist?); the "problem of free will"; the "problem of knowing other minds"; the "problem of the existence of God," et cetera, et cetera, long into the night. But these are not the questions of philosophy; they are only the fossilized remains of what were once living and breathing "creatures." Official philosophy, a sort of paleontology of the mind, lays out these bones and fragments and reconstructs gigantic skeletons called "philosophical arguments," which are housed in museums called philosophy departments and philosophy texts. But reconstruction is not remembering. The "problems of philosophy" are only the tracks left by the questions of philosophy—something that has long since moved on, and is still moving within every serious human being.

What is this quality of magic that is attached to real philosophy? I have seen it countless times in the faces of students venturing into philosophy classes for the first time. Speak to these same young people six months or a year later, or after they've left school.

Almost without exception, they have been bitterly disappointed. "I had the fantasy," says one, "that philosophy would teach me ultimate wisdom." Another shrugs and says, "I was unrealistic. My expectations were way out of line."

What expectations? And why "unrealistic"? How many times have I heard the same thing from people I now meet at lectures and conferences throughout the country? I am astounded by how many successful men and women in our society seriously studied philosophy in their youth. I don't mean those who took it only to satisfy some college requirement; I mean those who majored in it or who took considerably more than the required number of courses. Asked to speak about their studies of philosophy, they undergo a change. Suddenly their faces are young, and then, just as suddenly, they smile sadly or cynically.

Their numbers are truly astonishing. I feel as though I've uncovered a secret national love affair. Or, if I may put it this way, it is as though I've discovered that everyone has slept with the woman I married and, moreover, that she treated them all rather badly. It is not hard to see that these people are still carrying a torch.

Here is a businessman, the vice-president of a medical insurance company. He has come to a public lecture on bio-ethics in which I am one of the panelists. The main speaker, a public-health official, discusses the "right-to-choose" issue, particularly with respect to cancer treatment, and the other members of the panel afterwards bring up all sorts of other matters. A priest describes his work counseling the families of people with terminal illness. A physician weighs the evidence about the effectiveness of Laetrile. The philosopher (myself) asks about the modern medical attitude toward illness. I question this attitude in the light of Plato's teaching against the emotions that breed moral weakness by trapping man in the world of appearances. In the course of explaining this startling doctrine of Plato, I summarize the famous "allegory of the cave," in which Plato likens the human condition to that of prisoners chained in a cave, taking shadows for reality. After the discussion, the insurance executive approaches the platform. His eyes fall upon me and I watch him pausing in front of our table. Will he go to the health official to discuss the cost-effectiveness of insuring alternative systems of health care? Or will he choose to ask me something that has nothing at all to do with his business or professional concerns? He stands there, torn for a moment between two worlds, two aspects of himself. He chooses, finally, to speak to me and pours out thoughts and questions that have been lying half-starved in his mind for thirty years.

Here is a newspaper publisher, a dynamic, energetic man of forty, seated across from me at a dinner party. He begins to ask me about the level of public concern with new religious movements and about other related subjects that might be good material for feature stories, such as the claim by some scientists that the new physics is verifying the mystical doctrines of the Eastern religions. In the middle of explaining the Hindu doctrine of the cosmos as mind, I am amazed to see how quickly he sets aside all concern about selling papers and begins to argue against the mystical meta-physics of Hinduism. Before long, the whole table of ten people has sailed into the discussion and—to the tune of clinking glasses, china, and silverware—I am moderating a seminar on science and metaphysics. Partway through I give way to an impulse. I sit back, narrow my eyes, and imagine that the conversation is taking place in a foreign language. These attractive women, vigorous men leaning toward each other—what is going on here? What is causing this extraordinary animation? Yes, of course, it is after all a dinner party. And these people really do like each other and so any pretext for conversation is welcome.

But there is more involved, far more. Mrs. D., seated at the corner of the table, spends her days in auction houses and working as a volunteer for charitable projects; look at her now. She can't wait to put in her thoughts about the nature of the self! Helen F., at my right, a well-known attorney specializing in minority rights cases, has completely forgotten about her meal; her eyes are lowered; her brow is knotted; her right hand is clenched into a fist at her lips; she is reaching for a new thought—about what? And Jonathan S., our host, an eminent psychiatrist: He is speaking in a voice none of us (and we all know him well) has ever heard. He stumbles over words; his voice cracks—he looks at me questioningly; he apologizes for broken chains of thought and incomplete sentences—but there is something he wants to say, or rather ask, or is it rather propose, suggest—he doesn't know—about immortality of the soul! He is compelling because he is speaking from his search, not from his knowledge.

And, finally, here is a Catholic nun who has come to my office at the university. I first met her several years ago when I was writing my book on Christianity. We had several long talks about the traditions of spirituality and mysticism in the contemporary Church. She has been auditing my seminar on Pythagoras. She tells me she is coming to this class because she is seeking a new language for Christianity and she seems to hear it in our weekly discussions. This new language—what is it? It is *not* the language of religion, yet it touches her in a strangely powerful way. We talk. I know what she is reaching for, but I can't say it to her directly; I do not want to offend and I am really not sure if it is the same for everyone: There is something closer to oneself than religion, something greater than mysticism; more concrete and yet more unknown. There is an aspect of myself that is anterior to religion, that moves in another direction, that answers to nothing or to no one else but itself. When it is activated, I become quiet; I listen. It is not religious silence; it is not "sweet"; the mind is quiet, but very alive; everything that it knows is now in question, but without fear. In that moment some entirely new movement begins in me, new but strangely familiar; I sense the possibility of a breathtaking stability. I am attentive; I wait.

The process of remembering has begun.

How far this remembering will go it is impossible to say. But it has been initiated through contact with a language that has a specific "sound." I have seen it numerous times in students like this nun who come from the religions, even from the Eastern religions, even from Buddhism. It is true that the language of Buddhism is far more scientific and psychological than Western religious language. However in its contemporary form it no longer seems to touch that unknown part of the mind where a man senses both the terror and hope of a universe of law. Buddhism today has somehow acquired the general Western patina of acceptability— even in its most "esoteric" forms, such as Zen or Tibetan Buddhism. In any case, I have seen pupils who have practiced one or another form of Buddhism respond exactly like this nun to the language of authentic philosophy. The point is that not even the devoted practitioner of religion, be it conventional religion or a new religion—no one, I don't care how intense or sophisticated his spiritual practice; I don't care how naive or simplistic, how conventional or unorthodox—is ever quite prepared for the shock of real questioning. The young Zen Buddhist comes from his morning sitting in which he has attempted to abandon the hindrances of mind and "thinking." Yet in front of authentic philosophy, he is astonished to find that serious thought is actually the same thing as freedom from "thought."

It is exactly the same with scientists and young people of scientific bent. Suddenly, they realize that there exists a world of ideas—ideas which are of an astonishingly different quality from the concepts and theories of science, yet which retain the element of objectivity. They are being asked to use their mind, that mind that has led them through the problems of their scientific investigations—yet it is not the same mind, not the same part of the mind. They try with their scientific, familiar mind to answer the questions of philosophy, but it is not possible. (*It is not possible* to approach the questions of philosophy with the scientific/scholarly mind alone: that is what academic philosophy does not understand.) Some of them attempt to convert the questions to intellectual problems, but I know that at the other end of the problem they find the question still waits for them. At that point they are in exactly the same situation as those who have come from the religions. The state of questioning has brought everyone together. The scientist, the student of science, comes from his laboratory where he has attempted to abandon the hindrances of subjectivity and emotion in order to see the real world. In front of authentic philosophy, he is astonished to find that the emotion evoked in him by great ideas is actually the same thing as freedom from emotion.

The magic of real philosophy is the magic of the specifically human act of self-questioning—of being in front of the question of oneself. In using the analogy of being in love, I have not been merely literary. It is like love; it *is* love. How can that be? Why give the name "love," except by way of poetics, to this troubling interest in ideas such as truth, reality, being?

To answer this question, we may turn to Plato, who defined love as a striving, a seeking for that which is higher and greater than oneself. Such striving lies at the very core of the human psyche. But not only does man strive, not only *is* man a striving for immersion in absolute being, he also seeks consciousness of being, understanding of it.

Plato gave this longing a name: *eros*, the god of love. He allows the figure of Socrates to give voice to this idea of love; and Socrates, for his part, calls upon his own "teacher in the art of love," the mysterious Diotima. Love, she says, is a spiritual force (*daimon*) and, as such, belongs to the intermediate realm between heaven and earth, gods and mortals. Both in man and in the universe, in the microcosm and the macrocosm, there exists the world of the Intermediate, transmitting and receiving between levels of being. It is not simply that Plato sees the universe as "three-leveled"—earth, heaven, and the intermediate realm, the realm of the *daimon*, the link *(syndesmos)*. It is often put this way myth-ically in order to be felt—in order that the idea will guide man's conduct, rather than simply engage the activities of his intellectual faculties. Ideas cannot guide man's conduct, cannot point toward meaning, unless they are felt in the way and in the manner in which real feeling operates.

Thus we see the idea of the threefold nature of man and the universe diversely expressed throughout all cultures and nations: earth, heaven, and the intermediate movement—the "messengers of the gods"; the daemons in Western antiquity; the *dakinis* in Tibetan Buddhism; the Valkyrie of the Teutons; the angels in Judaism and Christianity. The threefold nature of the real world is a basic, fundamental idea that needs mythic expression in order to be felt, in order to guide human life. This threefold reality exists at all levels of being—and there are many levels. But the idea of many levels implies many triads, many degrees of "heaven-earth-daemon."

However, the teaching of many levels, many trinities, is an-other idea, a separate idea. Ancient philosophy, in the form of mythic reasoning, took one idea at a time. Heaven-earth-daemon, higher-lower-intermediate, is a *principle*; it needs to be absorbed in its simplicity—that is, in the part of the human mind that is basic and simple; in this way the ancient transmissions make it possible to take one idea at a time. It is quite another kind of thought that strives for complexity—or rather, complication. Complication of ideas is the result of a premature and impatient reaching for completeness. When philosophy falls prey to this impatience it begins to lose its real power in human life.

Here we are speaking of the one idea of the intermediate force in man and the universe, one of whose names is *love*, the striving for the higher *from beneath*. There are other names for the love that strives toward the lower *from above*: Hermes is the represen-tative of this kind of love, as was the ancient Egyptian god Thoth, bringing the teachings of wisdom to man from God. *Eros* itself is a force that operates in both directions. But the aspect of *eros* we are considering points upward, ever upward in the inner and outer cosmos.

> "What then is Love?" I asked. "Is he mortal?"
>
> "No."
>
> ". . . [He] is neither mortal nor immortal, but in a mean between the two."
>
> "What is he, Diotima?"
>
> "He is a great spirit *(daimon)*, and like all spirits he is intermediate between the divine and the mortal."
>
> "And what," I said, "is his power?"
>
> "He interprets," she replied, "between gods and men, conveying and taking across to the gods the prayers and sacrifices of men, and to men the commands of the gods and the benefits they return; he is the mediator who spans the chasm which divides them, and therefore by him the universe is bound together. . . . For God mingles not with man; but through Love all the intercourse and converse of gods with men . . . is carried on. The wisdom which understands this is spiritual; all other wisdom, such as that of arts and handicrafts is mean and vulgar. Now these spirits or intermediate powers are many and diverse, and one of them is Love."
>
> "And who," I said, "was his father, and who his mother?"
>
> "The tale," she said, "will take time . . ."*

To tell this "tale" is the principal aim of this book. The tale, the identification and strengthening of the philosophical impulse, has not yet been told in our present era. It is a tale about myself; it has not yet been told to me. But how to tell it now? What is

---

*Plato, *Symposium* 203, *The Dialogues of Plato*, 4th ed., trans. Benjamin Jowett (Oxford: Oxford University Press, 1953).

mythic reasoning for you and me? How to acknowledge the love of wisdom, the need for wisdom, without putting it in neon lights or serving it up predigested? How to avoid romanticizing the wish for truth? How to face the fact that great ideas are not by themselves enough and yet without them nothing is possible for us? The heart of philosophy is always breaking. Truth, ideas that come from a higher level, pass judgment on me—and on you, the reader. Do you think you can escape that?

"The tale," she said, "will take time; nevertheless I will tell you. On the day when Aphrodite was born, there was a feast of all the gods, among them the god Poros or Plenty, who is the son of Metis or Sagacity. When the feast was over, Penia or Poverty, as the manner is on such occasions, came about the doors to beg. Now Plenty, who was the worse for nectar . . . went into the garden of Zeus and fell into a heavy sleep; and Poverty considering that for her there was no plenty, plotted to have a child by him, and accordingly she lay down at his side and conceived Love [Eros], who partly because he is naturally a lover of the beautiful, and because Aphrodite is herself beautiful, and also because he was begotten during her birthday feast, is her follower and attendant. And as his parentage is, so also are his fortunes. In the first place he is always poor, and anything but tender and fair, as the many imagine him; and he is rough and squalid, and has no shoes, nor a house to dwell in; on the bare earth exposed he lies under the open heaven, in the streets, or at the doors of houses, taking his rest; and like his mother he is always in distress. Like his father too, whom he also partly resembles, he is always plotting against the fair and the good; he is bold, enterprising, strong, a mighty hunter, always weaving some intrigue or other, keen in the pursuit of wisdom, fertile in resources: a philosopher at all times, terrible as an enchanter, sorcerer, sophist. He is by nature neither mortal nor immortal, but alive and flourishing at one moment when he is in plenty, and dead at another moment in the same day, and again alive by reason of his father's nature. But that which is always flowing in is always flowing out, and so he is never in want and never in wealth; and, further, he is in a mean between ignorance and knowledge. The truth of the matter is this: No god is a philosopher or seeker after wisdom, for he is wise already; nor does any man who is wise seek after wisdom. Neither do the ignorant seek after wisdom. For herein is the evil of ignorance, that he who is neither good nor wise is nevertheless satisfied with himself; there is no desire when there is no feeling of want."*

We shall have many reasons to return to Plato and to his teaching about love and remembering. Before concluding this opening chapter let us find our way back to the world we live in, the twentieth century, the world of advanced technology, nuclear energy, television, computers, the crisis of ecology, energy, impending global war, the world in which all the patterns of living that have guided mankind over the millennia are breaking down— in the structure of the family, the nature of work and vocation, the indices of personal identity, social worth and service to others; in the meaning of wealth and poverty; in the compounding ambiguities of scientific research—the world of the present moment in time. This is the world we live in—the world of difficulties and problems, threats of unprecedented destruction, promises of unprecedented progress. For us, these crises, problems, and promises comprise *the world of appearances*. Among these appearances we experience our question, the question of the meaning and purpose of our lives.

*Symposium 203–204, trans. Jowett.

In the history of philosophy, the idea of *the world of appearances* refers to something rather different, something quite interesting, but not immediately relevant to the present need. The world of appearances, traditionally, is the world of *things*, external realities—tables, chairs, mountains, planets, plants and animals, other people—all that appears to the senses as an entity; the world in which we seem to live and move. Many philosophers, ancient and modern, have argued that this world of *things* is not what it seems at all; behind these *appearances* is another world, the real world, existing in and of itself, and we are wrong to believe in the ultimate reality of things we see and touch during the course of our lives.

The traditional philosophical puzzle is whether the *things* of this world are real or illusory. But that formulation is not directly relevant for us. Not things, but *situations* comprise the world we live in, the world that faces us and claims to be real. The situations and problems of our everyday life, the crises, the ambiguities themselves are *our* "world of appearances."

Behind *these* appearances there lies a real world of self-inquiry into which we need to penetrate. This real world is every bit as difficult of access as the mysterious noumenon of Kant, or the remote Platonic Forms. Like these higher worlds, it is closed to our ordinary mind and senses. This world also demands a different faculty of knowing—a power of the mind which Socrates sought to develop in man. It will be our task in this book to clarify what this power is, for it lies not in the ability to *know*, but in the ability to *ask*. Behind the problem, lies the Question.

CHAPTER 2

Socrates and the Myth of Responsibility

Regarded as though from outer space or from another dimension of time, human history presents a spectacle of the repeated failure of great ideas to penetrate the human heart. To list all the philosophical, religious, ethical, political, and psychological ideas that have been introduced into human society in two and a half millennia would be impossible. It is enough to call to mind only a few to become convinced that some pervasive misunderstanding seems to have haunted civilization from the very beginning—a misunderstanding that has prevented the influence of great ideas from acting beyond a certain point in the lives of the individual and the collective.

The ideals of the Judeo-Christian tradition, for example, remain an article of belief for millions and have been so for centuries. But neither Judaism nor Christianity can stand in relationship to the terrors of the twentieth century: the atrocities of global war and holocaust—mass torture and murder, the betrayal and destruction of whole cultures and nations; the ravaging of massive portions of the physical earth; the deceptions, lies, and bloodshed that began on a world scale in World War I and accelerated through World War II with the Nazi holocaust, the Russian programs of genocide, the American bombing and slaughter of the people of East Asia. The twentieth century is a record of forces and events emerging out of the depths of human life that completely baffle the philosophies of the Western religious tradition.

That such events should have happened at all is an over-whelming indictment of the philosophies of the Western world, their failure to have an influence on the deepest springs of human action. But granted that they have happened, there is not even an understanding of their nature by our philosophies. Our philosophy simply stands confused in front of them with utterly no relation-ship to them.

If this is true of the Judeo-Christian tradition, all the more is it true of other teachings that we know—from the philosophies of ancient Greece up to the latest teachings of modern science. Sooner or later all ideas about man and nature founder in front of some unexpected manifestation of the human unconscious that shocks, horrifies, and stupefies—manifestations alien to our sense of re-sponsibility. Whether the tough-minded theories of Marxism or Freudianism or the rationalist, humanist theories of the eighteenth century, sooner or later humanity manifests itself out of some unknown and alien depth in the form of a crime or outrage that casts all philosophy to the wind. No human being can take respon-sibility for this manifestation. Eventually a new philosophy is sought to account for this eruption of the human unconscious, and once again the myth of responsibility begins to form. Men imagine they know the general structure of man; the new philosophy seems to embrace the whole nature of man—his divinity and his animality, his fears and desires, his strengths and weaknesses. Then again the whole edifice crumbles in the face of a new outrage, a new atrocity or war. Out of the depths of fear, tension, and agitation, man once again manifests behavior incommensurate with the prevailing philosophy.

It is this fact of human life on earth, more than any other single element, that explains the sterility of the modern pursuit of philosophy and necessitates a completely new understanding of philosophical inquiry. Ideas do not raise the level of human life, not even great ideas, not even the ideas of Christ or Moses or Plato. They remain and have remained only ideas.

Ideas do not transform human life. Is this an inevitable law? Is mankind forever doomed to turn round and round in the same track while, seated on gorgeous whirling thrones, men of genius and good will fashion magnificent teachings and philosophies that have no real transforming power on the actual course of human life?

Must philosophy be powerless?

This way of putting the issue can be studied and verified by any individual who simply examines his own life. In one's own individual life the same drama is played out that is played out on the stage of world history. My individual sense of responsibility does not and cannot reach into the deep unconscious layers of the human structure. Every day, in almost every life, manifestations appear within myself for which I can have no responsibility. The place from which these manifestations arise has no relationship to the ideals I hold in my mind or heart. I produce my own atrocities, my own world wars, convulsions, attacks, revolutions. These manifestations are my emotions—especially, the negative emotions. Every day nearly every human being has evidence that his ideals and ideas do not reach into the unconscious parts of oneself. In fact, this is such a common experience that it is hardly noted by most of us; it's simply assumed to be quite in the nature of things.

The irony is that, with evidence staring us in the face every day that our philosophy does not penetrate into our own being, we continue to live under the assumption that we are responsible for ourselves. We live immersed in that assumption and teach it to our children. Our art is structured around this assumption— our sense of drama and meaning is based upon it; our religion is based upon it; our moral axioms are based upon it; our civil and criminal law and the whole structure of social and family life is based upon it. Yet it is a completely false assumption. Our sense of responsibility does not reach down to the core of our nature.

Philosophy in the Western world was actually born in the light of this perception about the powerlessness of the mind. It was Socrates' vision that neither the religion nor the science of his day was leading man to virtue—a term which had a specific meaning

associated with the power of mind in relationship to the unconscious parts of the human structure. Virtue, in this sense, was the
aim of human life for Socrates. The term "self-mastery" no longer
conveys this precise shade of meaning—namely, that the only aim
worthy of a human being is to create a channel of responsibility and relationship between truth, ideas, mind on the one hand,
and the unconscious structures of human nature on the other—
what we may call the emotional, instinctive aspect of the human
organism.

It is difficult to imagine the sort of impact that Socrates must
have made on those around him. One becomes so accustomed to
Socrates and Plato as historical figures that one sits back and just
accepts, without even a ripple of feeling, that one remarkable man
could have had so overwhelming an influence on the course of
human history throughout the millennia. Socrates? Oh, yes, I
know about him. He wandered the streets of Athens questioning,
probing, upsetting people's opinions about themselves and the
universe.

Let us try to call forth some more nearly authentic feeling
about this Socrates. To be the most influential mind even in one's
neighborhood or graduating class is not something entirely to be
scorned. But to be the most influential mind in Western history—
what could that mean? What kind of a being are we speaking
about?

First, let us realize that as the center of culture of the ancient
world, fifth-century Athens contained, in essence, every sort of
artistic, intellectual, and pragmatic current that we know of in our
own culture. We have modern science; ancient Greece had the
equivalent in the natural philosophers of the time—the equivalent
of our physicists, mathematicians, biologists. We have the religions of Christianity and Judaism; ancient Greece had its religions
as well, its gods, its orientation toward salvation, the other world,
its sacred rituals, its symbols, its spirituality. In short, Socrates
knew about religion—quite as much as you or I or anyone in our

world knows about religion. It counts as nothing to say that Socrates did not know about Christ and therefore was not exposed to the same depth of religious truth as modern man. It counts as nothing to say this, because of the quite obvious fact that very few, if any, human beings today can be said to know about Christ. In every culture in all times, there exists religion; and let us grant that Socrates understood, at the very least, the depths of the religious impulse.

Science and religion. Then as now. But to Socrates, nothing of science or religion could suffice. It was this one thing he fixed upon—this one factor of the powerlessness of the mind, which he called the absence of virtue—that Socrates considered the single and only factor of importance in human life. Socrates was not a religious teacher. Extraordinary! Socrates was not a scientific thinker. Also extraordinary! But what is most extraordinary of all—he was neither of these, nor was he any other recognizable kind of teacher! What was he? What was the source of his immense influence? And what does this notion of the responsibility of the mind in relationship to emotion and behavior, why does this almost easily understandable notion require for its exploration a man of such incredible stature and force; who is, above all, incomprehensible by any usual standards of religion and science. Again, the question: What was Socrates?

Socrates was neither science nor religion. Nor was he art—in any familiar sense of the word. He was not politics, in any familiar sense of the word. He questioned, interrogated—yes, this we can assume about him. Yet Socrates and the activity of Socrates, his questioning, is an unknown factor. This unknown factor, the force we cannot label or explain in terms familiar to us, exerted and continues to exert a current of influence throughout the world that has rarely been equaled and perhaps never surpassed in recorded history. What was Socrates? The point is: What was the Socratic questioning? If virtue was the aim of Socrates, why was it pursued through questioning rather than through the sort of exposition of doctrine, analysis of concepts, synthesis of great ideas, formation of symbols, monuments, works of music and art, legislation of political systems, or any of the countless modes and methods through which great minds have transmitted ideas over the centuries? To ask what was Socrates is to ask about the existence in man and in ourselves of a faculty of inquiry that is unknown under the names we give to the powers of the mind: It is not metaphysical speculation; it is not scientific analysis; it is not spiritual doctrine; it is not moral reasoning; it is not criticism. The result of this power of mind is not the establishment of a system of ideas, nor the organization of a school of thought, nor the founding of a religion or a state. The result is not the portrayal of noumenal realities, basic atoms of the world, fundamental concepts of God or being.

The Socratic power is to penetrate, again and again, behind the world of appearances; the world of emotional appearances as well as the world of perceptual appearances—that is, the world as I like it or dislike it, the world to which I am attached in my emotions, the world of my emotions. To penetrate beyond the world of appearances means to destroy my beliefs, my opinions, my certainties not only about objects, but about myself. What opens out beyond these appearances? Nothing—except a new quality of mind that stands for the moment in actual relationship to the unconscious parts of human nature. Beyond the appearance, lies the Question. To Socrates, the channel of virtue, the power of real philosophy lies somehow in this special power of self-interrogation.

Socrates is unknown. And he is great. These two aspects of the man must be kept in mind and turned over again and again until we begin to feel what is at issue here. It is not a matter of saying something new about the history of philosophy, of arguing that Socrates has been misunderstood and that the whole enterprise of philosophy itself is not simply, as Whitehead stated, a series of footnotes to Plato, but rather a series of misunderstandings of Socrates. What is at issue are the questions about life itself which every serious human being asks. At issue is the fact that when I hear the call of great ideas I also hear a part of myself of which I am usually unaware. At the same time, I see the chaos and violence of my own life and of the life of man on earth. Or I see the meaninglessness of it—its end in death or its perpetuation as a carousel of illusions. Ideas exist; meaning exists—call it God perhaps; God exists—but the higher reality that these words represent does not exist in myself as an effective material force in my life. I may love the greatness of truth; but by itself it does not change me. And it is material change—transformation—we are speaking of. What action, what movement in myself is necessary to pass the energy of truth into my own flesh and blood? The Socratic interrogation is not simply a project of asking about this issue; *the interrogation is itself a material, chemical process* by which the transformation begins to take place within oneself. This fact, and only this fact, can explain the greatness and mystery of Socrates. He questioned, but not as we question. His questioning created a channel within human nature for the reconciliation of mind and body, a channel of virtue or power.

Socrates existed, and for us Socrates is a metaphor of an activity of mind that defines what it means to be human. Socrates exists as a metaphor of the structure of man, of myself now and here and my possible development. Now and here, like Socrates, I am surrounded by scientific knowledge, by the remnants of great religious traditions, the surviving messages of exalted teachings, by symbols—broken and disfigured, but still retaining beauty and power. Like Socrates, I am surrounded by moralities and commandments—some echoing the greatness of ancient wisdom, others constructed only yesterday in order to accommodate some new forms of civilization; still others constructed just a moment ago for my own or others' comfort or egoistic profit. Like Socrates, I am met all the time by voices claiming this or that opinion to be truth, voices inside and outside myself. These interlocutors of Socrates are my own selves arising to claim they know. And yet I, too, live in Athens, that Athens of the fading light, crippled by a war, governed by corrupt spirits, immersed in changing opinions of what is good and true. Like Socrates, I am surrounded by inventions and artistic novelties—music, art, theater in all their varied forms. Art reflects a vision of harmony in which I go to rest and hope and to experience something of the state of mind that I long for. Yet, when I return to living, I see that my emotions have not been transformed; I see that there are higher emotions that appear when I am plunged in art or religion or philosophy, but these are not the emotions that appear when I undertake to live day to day with the people in my life or with the challenges that life offers me simply for survival, or for the sake of accomplishment, or in the face of pain, disappointment, disease, death.

No, like Socrates, I am compelled to question the emotions that art, philosophy, and morality instill and support in myself; these emotions are not the emotions that really drive my life. The latter, the emotions that really drive me and that cause the manifestations and actions of my life, appear like alien beings within my skin, capturing the whole of myself and leading me to be and act in ways totally incomprehensible to myself. Like St. Paul, I could cry out: "The good that I would do, that I do not; that which I hate, that do I." My responsibility does not penetrate into these manifestations. I have no virtue. Like Socrates, I have ideas— these citizens of Athens inside me—but they do not bring me virtue: the relationship between truth, mind, and my flesh and blood.

Socrates, real philosophy, begins with the confrontation of this situation in myself and in the whole of human life. I am alone; religion, science, art, morality—all these exist outside of myself. There is something in the mind that is my own, that cannot be claimed by religion, science, art, or morality. There is something in the mind that is free, autonomous. But what is it? It is Socrates the questioner—but questioning now as a force, not as a game of concepts; questioning as an act of attention.

It is here that we must recognize the existence also of Plato, that great pupil of the master. Historically, it is Plato who has given us Socrates in the monumental series of dialogues, the dialogues of Plato. Socrates wrote nothing down; historically, all we know of him is from a few extended treatments, chief of which are the Platonic dialogues, the memoirs of Xenophon, plus a handful of remarks and comments from contemporaries such as the comic playwright Aristophanes.

But we are not interested in the historical facts about Socrates; we are interested in the force of the Socratic consciousness as the real root of ourselves. Plato was a pupil—of this we can be historically certain and on this we can build our inquiry not into the facts of history, but into the facts of self-inquiry.

Plato was the pupil of Socrates. No greater, more all-encompassing set of ideas can be found than in the writings of Plato and in the influence of his philosophical system through the Platonic Academy, which persisted for hundreds of years after his death, and which gave rise to whole systems of thought around which the greatest intellects of the Western world organized themselves for two thousand years, even up until the present day. When the force of the Christian event began to articulate itself as a religion of the world, it was largely through the form and language of Platonic concepts. Plato plus Christianity equals ninety percent of the world we know and live in.

We will have ample opportunity to discuss the Platonic teachings further. But for now we must consider Plato principally as a result of Socrates. Plato, let us say, is the greatest speculative thinker in the history of the Western world. In intellectual depth he is Einstein. In artistic power he is the heir of great tragedians of ancient Greece and surely showed the sensitivity of a Dante or a Shakespeare—one has only to mention the *Apology*, the *Phaedo*, and the *Crito*, dialogues that, taken together, create the mythic

Socrates and engender in the reader, twenty-five hundred years later, the tears and joy of objective, universal feeling. As a social thinker he is a great lawgiver and theorist of social order, as evidenced in his greatest single work, the *Republic*, and as articulated in detail in his all-encompassing last work, *The Laws*; Plato is a creator of myth and symbol, a cosmologist whose work the *Timaeus* governed Western man's thought about the universe for over two thousand years. And perhaps even above all this, he is the greatest psychological theorist of Western history, offering a dynamic of inner life against the background of a clear articulation of the possible development of the human soul. As an ethicist, he is supreme.

Through Plato, ideas about the whole of life and reality entered the stream of what we call Western history, influencing every other mind in every other activity in the Western world, as well as in the Middle East where, conjoined with the inspired mentalities of the Islamic world, it also had its significance.

How to put it? Plato's thought encompasses the whole of human life in the Western world for twenty-five hundred years. So far-reaching is it that even the most profound minds of the Christian, Judaic, and Islamic revelations bowed before Plato; even the greatest scientific minds—Newton, Galileo, Kepler, Copernicus—bowed before Plato; kings, princes, and conquerors bowed before Plato, whether consciously or not; artists, builders, musicians bowed before Plato. In the Middle Ages when Aristotle (a pupil of Plato) was of such overwhelming influence, representing as he did the concentrated power of logic and empirical honesty, even then Plato's thought held sway indirectly, bursting forth again with undisputed power at the approach of the Renaissance, which means the approach of the contemporary era.

And yet Plato was the result of Socrates; the greatest system of ideas is the result of the great master of questioning and self-interrogation. Behind Plato, above Plato, stands Socrates. Behind all-encompassing thought stands the destruction of the tyranny of thought. Behind the successful mind stands the self-revelation of ignorance and emptiness. The Socratic questioning is an act of the mind unknown in the whole Platonic system, an act in which the energy of consciousness seeks to make tangible contact with the unconscious structures of human nature—instinct, emotion, and ordinary mental activities. Plato is the result of the concrete search for inner virtue embodied in the life and comportment of Socrates.

Let us say that Plato is the greatest speculative thinker that we know of in the history of our civilization. Yet Socrates is higher than Plato. Socrates represents a higher level of the mind; not a higher system of concepts, but *the activation of a different energy* within human nature. The history of the Western world is testimony that not even the greatest systems of ideas can create a contact between the mind and the unconscious parts of human nature. Thought is not virtue; another energy of the mind is required.

There is one special place in the Platonic writings where Plato describes the effect upon man of this higher level of mind. Throughout the dialogues he tells us again and again of the disturbing effect that Socrates has upon his hearers. In only one place, however, does Plato vividly portray the transforming power of this disturbance—the upheaval of self-interrogation which brings the unconscious parts of the psyche into contact with conciousness.

This description of the effect of self-seeing takes place in the *Symposium*, the same dialogue in which love is portrayed as the half-god, half-mortal Eros, striving for the eternal possession of beauty while aware of the lack and ignorance within. This love, this *eros*, is a feeling and knowing in which joy and remorse are conjoined, a knowledge of value and good which is conjoined to the awareness of one's own egoism. The English word for this aspect of love is *conscience*. Here in the *Symposium* we are informed that the Socratic interrogation is far more than the investigation of ideas and concepts—that Socrates does more than confute opinions in the intellectual sense. We are made to realize that

Socrates awakens something in man, a sort of fire, which alone can bridge the separate parts of human nature and create moral power.

It occurs at the end of the *Symposium* with the raucous entrance of the figure of Alcibiades. But before describing this remarkable passage, let us pause to view again this whole question of responsibility or virtue—responsibility as a relationship between consciousness and the unconscious parts of human nature. We need to be sure we understand what we are speaking about. To that end, it will be helpful to call to mind some of the language that has been used over the centuries to refer to this contact between the parts of human nature, and to see how this language has become drained of force and meaning.

The mastery of desire is one of the phrases that has echoed through the ages when virtue is at issue. It is a phrase badly in need of retranslation and restatement, all the more since Freud persuaded people that (1) the strongest desires in man cannot be seen; (2) since they cannot be seen they cannot be mastered; (3) even if they could be seen and mastered, it would be a mistake to do so, since mastery of desire results in a general pathology due to suppressed energies that must inevitably manifest themselves in some form or other.

The Freudian earthquake completely destroyed the traditional concepts of reason and desire that had guided the moral life of Western man since the Middle Ages and the Renaissance. But Freudianism destroyed these concepts only because they had already been rebuilt on shaky foundations. Long before Freud the whole notion of a *ruling principle* within the mind had been reduced to a caricature of the ancient meaning. Freud saw that instead of reason actually ruling the passions, what was happening in the mind was only self-deception and internal compulsion based on the mechanical internalization of surrounding opinions about good and evil, a process which he lumped under the term "superego." Virtue, Freud taught, simply does not exist.

Modern people were at first unwilling to accept this concept, but were won over to it because in so explaining the internal workings of the mind, Freud was bringing the study of man into harmony with the scientific view of nature. Just as scientism has removed value from the outer world of nature, so Freud removed the organ of valuation from the inner world of man.

But Freud's theory of the superego, although acting like an earthquake, was in fact only the next logical step in the corruption of the whole distinction between reason and desire that had taken place in the centuries preceding him. The ancient, inner teaching about the mastery of desire had nothing to do with the destruction or suppression of biological and social impulses in man. Desire in its negative meaning was understood as the *absorption* of the finer energies of consciousness by the biological and social impulses. Desire was not understood as those impulses or emotions themselves. This process of absorption took place passively, unconsciously, and led to the formation of a false sense of oneself (egoism) and to manifestations, behavior, and further impulses (adding up to an illusory sense of "will") that are universally recognized as immoral—that is, injurious to others and destructive of the communal fabric.

Long before Freud, the religious moralists of the West increasingly enjoined man to battle against the results of this unconscious absorption of psychic energy, rather than against the cause of the emotions—the process of absorption itself. Generally, nothing can be done about these results, the egoistic emotions, except to suppress them or to substitute other egoistic emotions for them. The followers of Freud seem not to have understood the internal dynamics of the formation of these emotions and, in this, they perpetuated centuries of distorted psychology that had proceeded under the designation of the term "Christianity."

In sum, what are conventionally recognized as the desires, the emotions, or the passions in man are the effect of something more subtle and fundamental that takes place in the psyche prior to their formation. This subtle and fundamental process by which the finer energies of the mind are degraded into the egoistic emotions is the real unconscious enemy of man, and it is this unconscious process that the ancient inner teachings designated by the word *desire*. Not seeing or knowing about this process, Freudianism merely promulgated an ingenious theory about the formation of emotions based on the hypotheses of Darwinian biology.

To make a long story short, modern psychology was as incapable as "Christianity" had become of leading man to a liberating confrontation with desire or the process of the formation of egoistic emotions. This liberating, transformative confrontation may be designated by the word *conscience*, though the meaning of that term, too, may need to be rediscovered. When it is said that the sense of the responsibility does not reach down to the unconscious manifestations of our nature, what is meant is that there is no contact, no confrontation between the attention of the mind and the process of desire.

In order for this confrontation to occur and hence in order that conscience may be activated, there needs to take place in man a special sort of inner struggle. This struggle is what Socrates taught and exemplifies; this struggle is self-interrogation. It is not introspection; it is not insight; it is not emotional realization; it is not self-manipulation; it is not the formation of theories about oneself; it is not self-moralizing; it is not religious resolve. Similarly, Socrates is not science, not psychology (in our sense), not natural science, not art, not religion, not political action. Socrates is invisible to all these enterprises—incomprehensible, and perhaps even frightening to them. Self-interrogation is likewise invisible to ordinary thinking, feeling, and "willing." And conscience can be frightening to these more familiar aspects of our self as is no other force within us.

Alcibiades, then. In Plato's *Symposium* a series of speeches has been given in praise of love, ending with Socrates' characterization of love which we have already cited—love as the intermediate force in man moving between levels of being in the universe and in oneself. Eros, the love of truth and beauty, is half-god and half-mortal, in contact with both evil and the good at the same time. And the aim of this striving, called *eros*, is to merge with reality itself, beauty and goodness themselves, in order to conceive and give birth to virtue and wisdom in the soul. Enter Alcibiades.

Historically, Alcibiades was a rising member of the old Athenian aristocracy. He is pictured as a young man of exceptional good looks, intelligence, licentiousness, and ambition. Plato has him noisily entering the *Symposium* at the head of a drunken band of friends. He staggers in, supported on the arms of his companions, and proceeds to deliver a speech not about love as such, but about Socrates.

Socrates, he says, is like the statuettes of Silenus that are sold in the marketplace. The god Silenus was prince of the satyrs, offspring of Pan, and the constant companion of Dionysos. He was generally depicted as a bald, dissolute old man with a flattened nose, and with the hooves and horns of the class of *silenoi* or satyrs who seduce human beings through the beauty of their flute-playing. But Silenus, ugly as he was on the outside, was also regarded as an inspired prophet and the statues of him, to which Alcibiades refers, were hollow inside and contained miniature figures of the other gods. Alcibiades also compares Socrates to Marsyas, another notorious satyr, who boldly challenged Apollo himself at playing the pipes:

> You can't deny yourself, Socrates, that you have a striking physical likeness to both of these, and you shall hear in a moment how you resemble them in other respects. . . . But you don't play the flute, you will say. No, indeed; the performance you give is far more remarkable. Marsyas needed an instrument in order to charm men by the power which proceeded out of his mouth, a power which is still exercised by those who perform his melodies. . . . But you,

Socrates, are so far superior to Marsyas that you produce the same effect by mere words without any instrument. At any rate, whereas we most of us pay little or no attention to the words of any other speaker, however accomplished, a speech by you or even a very indifferent report of what you have said stirs us to the depths and casts a spell over us. . . . I myself, gentlemen, were it not that you would think me absolutely drunk, would have stated on oath the effect which his words have had on me, an effect which persists to the present time. Whenever I listen to him my heart beats faster than if I were in a religious frenzy, and tears run down my face, and I observe that numbers of other people have the same experience. Nothing of this kind ever used to happen to me when I listened to Pericles and other good speakers; I recognized that they spoke well, but my soul was not thrown into confusion and dismay by the thought that my life was no better than a slave's. That is the condition to which I have often been reduced by our modern Marsyas, with the result that it seems impossible to go on living in my present state. You can't say that this isn't true, Socrates. And even at this moment, I know quite well that, if I were prepared to give ear to him, I should not be able to hold out, but the same thing would happen again. He compels me to realize that I am still a mass of imperfections and yet persistently neglect my own true interests by engaging in public life. So against my real inclination I stop up my ears and take refuge in flight, as Odysseus did from the Sirens; otherwise I should sit here beside him till I was an old man. He is the only person in whose presence I experience a sensation of which I might be thought incapable, a sensation of shame; he, and he alone, positively makes me ashamed of myself. The reason is that I am conscious that there is no arguing against the conclusions that one should do as he bids, and yet that, whenever I am away from him, I succumb to the temptations of popularity. So I behave like a runaway slave and take to my heels, and when I see him the conclusions which he has forced upon me make me ashamed. Many a time I should be glad for him to vanish from the face of the earth, but I know that, if that were to happen, my sorrow would far outweigh my relief. In fact, I simply do not know what to do about him.*

The impact of Socrates is to produce upon a man a specific sort of suffering that involves seeing oneself against a very high criterion of what man should be. But this seeing of oneself is not a moralistic effort to persuade oneself to do better. On the contrary, its effect is to kindle *eros*, a longing for being. The impact of Socratic interrogation, which is objective self-interrogation, is the suffering that results from the repeated and prolonged confrontation in oneself between what one is meant to be and what one is. Until a man passes through this fire all his efforts at virtue will fail.

The perception of what I ought to be is more than a thought charged with emotional tension—which more or less defines the pathological phenomenon of guilt that Freud summarized by the term "superego." That it is far more than this is emphasized in the remainder of Alcibiades' speech. "This," Alcibiades continues, "is the effect which the 'piping' of this satyr has had on me and many other people. But listen and you shall hear how in other respects too he resembles the creatures to which I compared him, and how marvelous is the power which he possesses."

Alcibiades proceeds to tell of how he once tried to seduce Socrates, amorously. It should be noted that the existence of homosexuality among the upper classes in Athens generally has a meaning, in Plato, that is unrelated to the issue as it has taken

---

*Plato, *Symposium* 215–216, trans. Walter Hamilton (Harmondsworth, Middlesex: Penguin Classics, 1951), pp. 100–102.

form in the contemporary scene. In the Platonic dialogues, the question of love between men serves as a means for distinguishing the two kinds of friendship of which human beings are capable. The one kind of friendship is mutual assistance in the search for truth; the other kind is the mutual support of human weaknesses: "the friendship of men and the friendship of pigs."* As Plato writes about it, love between men is that impulse in human relationships which can be higher (nobler) than normal sexual love, that relationship in which the common aim is the movement toward being; or which can be lower than normal sexual love, in which individuals strengthen each other's faults, such as vanity, self-pity, fear, and laziness.

To continue, then, with the speech of Alcibiades and the portrayal of how Socrates ignites the fire of conscience, the confrontation of the two natures of man, in those who come near him:

> The Socrates whom you see has a tendency to fall in love with good-looking young men, and is always in their society and in ecstasy about them. Besides, he is, to all appearances, universally ignorant and knows nothing. But this is exactly the point in which he resembles Silenus; he wears these characteristics superficially, like the carved figure, but once you see beneath the surface you will discover a degree of self-control of which you can hardly form a notion, gentlemen. Believe me, it makes no difference to him whether a person is good-looking—he despises good looks to an almost inconceivable extent—nor whether he is rich nor whether he possesses any of the other advantages that rank high in popular esteem; to him all these things are worthless, and we ourselves of no account, be sure of that. He spends his whole life pretending and playing with people, and I doubt whether anyone has ever seen

*This pungent way of distinguishing the two kinds of friendship is attributed to G. I. Gurdjieff.

the treasures which are revealed when he grows serious and exposes what he keeps inside. However, I once saw them. . . .

Believing that he was serious in his admiration of my charms, I supposed that a wonderful piece of good luck had befallen me; I should now be able, in return for my favors, to find out all that Socrates knew; for you must know that there was no limit to the pride that I felt in my good looks. With this end in view I sent away my attendant, whom hitherto I had always kept with me in my encounters with Socrates, and left myself alone with him. . . . I naturally supposed that he would embark on conversation of the type that a lover usually addresses to his darling when they are *tête-à-tête*, and I was glad. Nothing of the kind; he spent the day with me in the sort of talk which is habitual with him, and then left me and went away. Next I invited him to train with me in the gymnasium. . . . He took exercise and wrestled with me frequently, with no one else present, but I need hardly say that I was no nearer my goal. . . . So I invited him to dine with me, behaving just like a lover who has designs upon his favorite. He was in no hurry to accept this invitation, but at last he agreed to come. The first time he came he rose to go away immediately after dinner, and on that occasion I was ashamed and let him go. But I returned to the attack, and this time I kept him in conversation after dinner far into the night, and then, when he wanted to be going, I compelled him to stay, on the plea that it was too late for him to go.

So he betook himself to rest, using as a bed the couch on which he had reclined at dinner, next to mine, and there was nobody sleeping in the room but ourselves. . . .*

Here Alcibiades interrupts his story to repeat his characterization of the inner state which Socrates creates in him. He has been

*_Symposium_ 217, trans. Hamilton, pp. 102–104.

"bitten," he said, in the most painful and sensitive part of any human being. "I have been wounded and stung in my heart or soul or whatever you like to call it by philosophical talk."* And he goes on to relate how he maneuvered himself into lying beside Socrates and "threw his arms around this 'truly superhuman and wonderful man.' " And thus he remained the whole night long. Yet Socrates "had the insolence, the infernal arrogance, to laugh at my youthful beauty and jeer at the one thing I was really proud of . . . and believe it, gentlemen, or believe it not, when I got up the next morning I had no more *slept* with Socrates, within the meaning of the act, than if he'd been my father or an elder brother."**

> What do you suppose to have been my state of mind after that? On the one hand I realized that I had been slighted, but on the other I felt a reverence for Socrates' character, his self-control and courage; I had met a man whose like for wisdom and fortitude I could never have expected to encounter. The result was that I could neither bring myself to be angry with him and tear myself away from his society, nor find a way of subduing him to my will. . . . I was utterly disconcerted, and wandered about in a state of enslavement to the man the like of which has never been known. †

Alcibiades goes on to tell of what he then saw of Socrates' character in two military campaigns—at Potidea and Delium. He saw a man of immense and unparalleled bravery, strength, and calm, as well as a man given on occasion to mysterious periods of

---

Symposium 218, trans. Hamilton, p. 105.
**Plato, *Symposium* 219, *The Collected Dialogues of Plato*, eds. Edith Hamilton and Huntington Cairns; trans. Michael Joyce, Bollingen Series, no. 71 (New York: Pantheon Books, 1964), p. 570.
†*Symposium* 219, trans. Hamilton, p. 107.

stillness and inner listening. To what was Socrates attending in these periods when he would stand unmoving in the midst of all the activity about him? The answer is given, or rather hinted at, elsewhere in the Platonic writings: In times of difficulty, Socrates turns his attention with extraordinary concentration to his own inner *daimon*, his inner god: conscience.* Concerning this "inner voice," Plato has Socrates speak of how few are the men who have access to it.** Yet it is precisely this power, this openness, this act of *remembering*, to which Socrates is leading those who can bear to stay with him. Socrates is far more than an interrogator who exposes illusions; he is also a presence, a personal force, who through his interaction with the other awakens in him the taste of conscience and inner divinity, a powerful, bittersweet awareness of two opposing movements within the human psyche: the inner slavery to the ego and the inner freedom of self. The being of Socrates transmits the taste of the higher; the interrogation of Socrates brings awareness of one's corruption and illusions.

And thus Alcibiades concludes by referring to both the person and the discourse of Socrates, who, he says,

. . . is so extraordinary, both in his person and in his conversation, that you will never be able to find anyone remotely resembling him . . . unless you go beyond humanity altogether, and have recourse to the images of Silenus and satyr which I am myself using in this speech. They are as applicable to his talk as to his person . . . his talk too is extremely like the Silenus-figures which take apart. Anyone who sets out to listen to Socrates talking will probably find his conversation utterly ridiculous at first, it is clothed in such curious words and phrases, the hide, so to speak, of a hectoring satyr. He will talk of pack-asses and black-

*Apol. 40a–c; Euthy. 3b; Rep. 496c; Phaedr. 242b.
**Republic, 496c.

smiths, cobblers and tanners, and appear to express the
same ideas in the same language over and over again, so
that any inexperienced or foolish person is bound to laugh
at his way of speaking. But if a man penetrates within and
sees the content of Socrates' talk exposed, he will find that
there is nothing but sound sense inside, and that this talk
is almost the talk of a god, and enshrines countless repre-
sentations of ideal excellence, and is of the widest possible
application; in fact that it extends over all the subjects with
which a man . . . needs to concern himself.*

In the entire corpus of the Platonic writings the figure of Alcibiades stands out as the man *in between*. All the other interlocutors
are generally unequivocally for or against Socrates; Alcibiades alone
feels what is true but sees that he cannot move toward it. Alcibiades alone is a man who is himself in question and, in that
respect, although he is portrayed as running away from Socrates and going on perhaps to a life of utter dissolution, he may be
taken as the most authentic pupil of Socrates in the Platonic
dialogues.

Was it Plato's intention to cast him in this light? It is difficult to
say, although the importance of the figure of Alcibiades is attested
by the existence of two other dialogues bearing his name: *Alcibiades I* and *Alcibiades II*. Whether these two shorter pieces were
actually written by Plato or by students of the Academy he founded
is a matter of scholarly dispute. But from our point of view the
historical problems are not critical. For us the importance of the
speech of Alcibiades lies elsewhere. It provides us with a measure,
a standard of what it means to penetrate behind the world of
appearance.

Facing the situations and problems of life, we are not going to
be seeking the age-old chimera of "things-in-themselves" in the

Symposium 222, trans. Hamilton, pp. 110–11.

sense of hard entities that exist independent of human perception. We are looking for a quality of questioning that both exposes our illusions and reminds us of what we ourselves really are and are meant to be. The Question is our Socrates—within a certain scale and limit. To be authentic it has to shake the mind and heart in ways that parallel the impact of Socrates upon Alcibiades, bringing both sides of our nature into view.

Within a certain scale and limit: That means of course that the real awakening of conscience requires the action upon us of a flesh-and-blood guide and the situations his presence can create. Can thought, our own thought, reproduce the Socratic shock, however faintly? Can we question our world and ourselves in such a way that sensitizes us to the need for conscience—in a completely new meaning of that word?

We are seeking an orientation toward life that can make individual moral responsibility a fact rather than a myth. Socrates, the flesh-and-blood guide, is not in front of me to lead me into "temptation" and "deliver me from evil"—creating situations and challenges that destroy my egoistic illusions while radiating the force of a higher level of being and good. Without the flesh-and-blood guide, can I discover the autonomous power of self-interrogation that can reach down into all the unconscious parts of my nature, can I at least touch the contours of this mental act that is the beginning of virtue?

I take it to be the aim of philosophy to bring man toward the struggle for conscience in the sense described. It can be called "remembering" in that conscience is more intimately myself than anything else in me; it can be called "remembering" in that a contact is made with a force such that when it appears, and only when it appears, I recognize that everything I have understood to be myself has not been myself.

What can take the place of Socrates in my life?

Historically and metaphorically the issue can be expressed in terms of a problem about the person of Socrates. Plato allows him to present himself as *a man who does not know*, whose "wisdom" consists in the fact that he alone of all the Athenians realizes his own ignorance. This is the root of the famous Socratic "irony." It is a lie in broad daylight—everyone sees through it, including the reader twenty-five hundred years later.

What is the teaching behind the Socratic silence, the Socratic power of self-interrogation? There must have been ideas about man and the universe behind this power—ideas far, far beyond the quality of mere theories, concepts, and explanations. The Socratic silence is higher than "knowledge"—this we have already seen. But there must have been behind this silence, this "ignorance," a knowledge-not-in-quotation-marks.

The point is obvious to anyone who has attempted serious self-observation. Without real ideas to guide the attention from within, the study of oneself soon reaches an insurmountable barrier created in part by the thoughts and concepts that are conditioned into the mind by the surrounding culture or subculture. Ideas are necessary in order to become free from concepts. Incarnated in a great teacher, great ideas become pure energy and love—the teacher acts and lives the ideas; they are his being. The teacher *is* his knowledge.

But no man begins the struggle for self-knowledge and self-transformation in this way, in this state of being. And so the question insists itself: What is the knowledge, the ideas, behind the Socratic method of life? It is more than the fascinating historical problem of who or what was Socrates' teacher. It is nothing less than the question of how we ourselves are to begin the long, serious journey of self-inquiry under the guidance of real knowledge.

We are asking: Are there ideas that can take the place of Socrates for myself here and now? Are there ideas that have the power to make us still and bring the whole of ourselves into question? Ideas that can help us begin the work of interrogation by means of which we penetrate behind the appearances of the crises and problems in which we are all enmeshed? Ideas that call us to the search for conscience in ourselves?

Behind Plato stands the immensity of Socrates. What greatness, what immensity stands behind Socrates himself? What ideas can help us begin the real work of inquiry?

We turn now to Pythagoras.

CHAPTER 3

Pythagoras

Was he the first and greatest scientific genius of the Western world? Was he a man of preternatural wisdom and psychic power, a master of the laws of consciousness and a spiritual guide to thousands? An incarnation of God? Or was he only an extraordinary combination of mathematician and mystagogue, an occultist, a "magician"?

All this and much more has been said of Pythagoras. Part man, part legend, the historical person is enveloped in uncertainty. Born in Asia Minor, perhaps in the year 569 B.C., he passed his early life on the island of Samos and is said to have flourished in 530 B.C. during the reign of the tyrant Polycrates. He seems to have left Samos to escape from the tyranny and to have settled in Croton in southern Italy, where, it is said, he rose to a position of great authority. His society came under attack in the year 500 B.C. and, after many wanderings in Italy, Pythagoras died at a ripe old age at Metapontium. It is said by some that he passed his middle years in Egypt studying the great knowledge and was taken to Babylon as a hostage when the Persian king, Kambyses, invaded Egypt. In Babylon, so the legend goes, he was also instructed in the teachings of the Zoroastrians.

Like Socrates, Pythagoras wrote nothing, or, if he did, nothing of it has survived the centuries. But unlike the case of Socrates, Pythagoras had no Plato, no contemporary pupil who systematized his teachings into formulations and arguments. The principal historical documents about the man and his teaching date from no less than eight hundred years after he lived and are mainly collections of stories and legends of questionable literal accuracy. These principal biographies do not offer much to the historian in search of facts about the external details of Pythagoras' life nor to the scholar in search of straightforward information about his ideas. But they are of great value as indications about the nature of awakening ideas and the manner in which they are transmitted.

This question of the transmission of ideas is absolutely central. Its neglect has bred tremendous confusion and prejudice throughout modern history and is one of the main reasons that philosophy has fallen to so low an estate in modern times. More, the neglect of this issue is a principal cause of the fact that reasoning and knowledge themselves have lost their moral power in our lives.

A consideration of the towering figure of Pythagoras will show us that there are two fundamental types of ideas. The first type may be regarded as a sort of energy, a higher energy that can, under very exact conditions, enter into the life of man with transforming effect. The energy of such ideas has been spoken of in ancient language as a spiritual food, the "manna from heaven" of the Old Testament. The verbal formulation of these ideas is only one aspect, though of course an important aspect, of the conditions necessary for the transmission of the energy they contain. The other conditions are many and varied, including certain forms of communal relations and the employment of many different kinds of symbolic methods—art, architecture, music, dance; as well as a certain orientation toward the needs of the body with respect to diet, sex, sleep, physical work, vocation, and numerous other factors. Here the verbal, conceptual formulation of ideas is only one element in a remarkable sort of overall existential training in which a greater energy is assimilated in the developing human being.

Nevertheless, these formulations, although they are only one aspect of the process by which man works for transformation, have a unique role in this process, especially in a culture where the development of intellect assumes a dominant role—a culture such as our own and such as existed in ancient Greece. This unique role we have already identified when we considered the impact of Socratic questioning. The authentic formulation of great ideas has the effect of bringing a man to silence, of stopping the mind. That is to say, the formulations of great ideas can create in us the state of self-questioning. "Only when thoughts are stopped can real thinking begin."

This oracular-sounding statement will be developed as we proceed with our discussion of Pythagoras. But let us now consider the second type of ideas. And let us begin by giving them a different name: concepts. Concepts require little more than careful verbal formulation in order to be communicated. They are, as it were, messages from the intellect to the intellect. To be understood, they require the analytic and combinatory powers of the mind, functions which are now being duplicated with increasing success by computers. In fact, one of the most important lessons that the technological revolution is now offering modern man is the realization of the automatic quality of those mental processes which he had hitherto identified as aspects of his freedom. This, too, we shall have to look at more closely in later chapters. The scientific world is a great bringer of questions—in its way a great "teacher" about ourselves and our illusions. But it functions as such only if we find a certain attitude toward the remarkable products of modern science, and only if we possess the necessary *ideas* (not concepts) that can guide this attitude.

Concepts are, so to speak, problem-solving devices, the internal equivalent of technologies; they are the technologies of the mind-machine. Concepts, theories, hypotheses, distinctions, comparisons—all these may be taken ultimately as instruments for organizing perceptions into logically consistent patterns called explanations. But they do not and cannot awaken in man a new quality of feeling or perceiving, a new organ or faculty of awareness. Concepts are no more nor less than tools by which man combines or analyzes that which he already knows through perceptions. If man's perceptions are limited mainly to the external senses, concepts can do no more than organize the material collected by the senses. Concepts can never reach beyond the level of perception or awareness at which man lives. Ideas, on the other hand, evoke, support, and require a higher level of awareness itself.

The great contribution of modern Anglo-American philosophy has been to expose the nature and limitations of concepts and conceptual thought. The sterility of this philosophy stems only from its unwarranted assumption that ideas are the same thing as concepts. In modern philosophy the basic metaphysical and moral questions of human life are often treated as meaningless locutions, confusions of language, fantasies, even "illnesses." And there is something tellingly true about this approach because for many centuries preceding our own the great questions of philosophy had degenerated into the confusion of ideas and concepts. No wonder modern man could never solve the problem of free will, or the problem of the existence of God, or the problem of the relationship between mind and body. Long before the rise of contemporary scientific, logical philosophy, ideas began to be treated as concepts, as problem-solving devices. When this happens, when it is forgotten that real ideas require not only intellectual attention, but an all-round moral effort in order to be grasped, then a hopeless confusion sets in compounded of ingenious metaphysical, ethical, or logical theories dealing with questions that actually require the activation within man of an entirely new energy of mind, an entirely new state of consciousness.*

Modern Anglo-American philosophy is quite correct in diagnosing the pathology of "philosophizing." Starting with the eighteenth-century Scottish philosopher David Hume and proceeding

---

*See Plato's allegory of the cave in the *Republic*. The prisoners can see only the shadows cast upon the wall in front of them. They are so shackled that they cannot see the real objects behind them merely by turning their heads. They must turn the whole body, the whole person, in order to see the reality that is directly behind them.

up to the twentieth-century philosophers Wittgenstein, Russell, Ayer, and many others, metaphysical speculation came to be identified as an exercise in futility. Just as Freud, Nietzsche, and Marx compellingly exposed the hypocrisies of modern European Judeo-Christian doctrines and forms, so contemporary scientific philosophy exposed the confusions of modern European metaphysical thought. But just as Freud, Nietzsche, and Marx were acquainted only with religious forms that had long since lost their real energy, so philosophers like Hume, Wittgenstein, and Russell were acquainted only with ideas whose formulations had long since lost their awakening force. Just as religion had been replaced by systems of rigid belief and oppressive moral fantasies, so philosophical ideas had been replaced by abstractions and concepts designed solely to solve problems of the intellect.

For many centuries, therefore, the life of Western civilization has been conducted in an ever-thickening atmosphere of concepts, theories, and hypotheses which were neither outwardly practical nor inwardly awakening. Questions concerning God, immortality, authentic morality, human identity were surrounded by the dead skin of great ideas—formulations that no longer served the purpose of guiding the act of self-interrogation, by which act alone such questions can be faced.

We need to find a proper name for this dubious offspring of ideas and concepts. How shall we designate these queer entities that superficially resemble their "parents," but which actually share none of their parents' real characteristics—yet which have exercised and continue to exercise such a harmful influence in our lives? What to call these mental formations that neither support inner questioning nor solve external problems, that serve neither the evolution of consciousness in man nor his immediate material survival in the world?

There are two reasons why I am concerned about correct terminology here. In the first place, both ideas and concepts are equally necessary to the life and development of man. Each has its proper sphere of activity corresponding to the two natures of man himself, the two worlds he is destined to inhabit by his very structure. Ideas move man toward the confrontation of his two natures by their power to support the act of total self-interrogation. Concepts, on the other hand, are mental mechanisms enabling man to function outwardly in the struggle with the specific challenges of external nature and social reality. A careless choice of terminology to designate the confusion of ideas and concepts may cause us to confer an excessive value on one or another part of human nature.

In the second place, it is necessary to keep in mind the fact that the abuse of the automatic mechanisms of thought cannot be eliminated by yet other automatic mechanisms—which is the main error of modern philosophy. The intellect's interference in the development of our lives is of such an immense importance and demands such a radical "cure" that the very word used to speak of it must touch not only the intellect but also the heart. The ancient inner traditions made use of mythic and symbolic expressions— "demons," "fallen angels," "dragons," "monsters"—that communicated the evil of approaching ultimate (sacred) questions with the wrong part of ourselves, and the dimensions of the struggle needed to resist this tendency.

As the invention of such a symbol is beyond my powers, I can only propose that we speak of these hybrids as *conceptualized ideas*. Although this term has no mythic or symbolic power, it can at least remind us, whenever we use it, of the existence of real ideas. For the purposes of definition, we may say that conceptualized ideas appear when the formulations of real ideas are treated solely or mainly as concepts, as principles or mechanisms for organizing data received through the senses in our ordinary state of consciousness. They therefore foster the illusion that the fundamental questions of life can be approached and even solved by one small part of the human psyche—the isolated intellect. And they foster the further illusion that ultimate truths about man and the universe can penetrate into the unconscious emotional and instinctive parts of ourselves without a long, difficult, and carefully guided inner struggle.

This terminology therefore enables us to speak more specifically about our pervasive inability to live according to what we believe to be the truth—about God or reality or our moral obligations. The point is that *conceptualized ideas cannot be assimilated into the whole of ourselves*. On the other hand, the primary function of real ideas is to bring a unifying energy into the whole structure of human nature. As for authentic concepts, which organize the data of external experience, they do not need to be assimilated by the whole person; that is not what they are for.

Finally, we can begin drawing the distinction between real philosophy and "philosophizing," and we can—without fear of insulting anyone—return the word "philosophy" to its rightful owners after its many centuries of exile. What proceeds under that exalted name in modern times may be spoken of now simply as conceptual analysis. To put it schematically, real philosophy degenerates into "philosophizing," which in turn is cured or destroyed by conceptual analysis. Similarly, within ourselves, real ideas degenerate into conceptualized ideas—but here the "cure" is rather more complex, involving, as it does, the educational *therapaeia* of persons and not only of systems of thought. Thus Socrates also engages in conceptual analysis, but only with the far greater aim of igniting the act of total self-questioning.

Who is the rightful "owner" of the word *philosophy?* It is none other than Pythagoras, and not only because historically it was he who coined the term.* It is necessary to understand *why* he invented this word.

To understand why Pythagoras introduced the new word *philosophy* into the language of the Greeks, we need only refer to our

---

*See Peter Gorman, *Pythagoras* (London: Routledge and Kegan Paul, 1979), p. 38.

discussion of love. Philosophy is the love of wisdom, not the possession of it. Philosophy is the striving to attain to the state in which the energy of truth, or real ideas, penetrates into one's flesh and blood, as well as one's mind.

The importance of this definition of philosophy cannot be overstated. Pythagorean ideas are not concepts. They were not transmitted in the manner of concepts; their action upon the mind of man was not the action of concepts. It is no doubt true that soon after the death of Pythagoras, and perhaps during his life as well, the ideas he brought (from where? from Egypt?) were spoiled by others and became what is historically known as Pythagoreanism. But this is only to repeat what we have already stated about the fate of real ideas in insufficiently prepared minds: Real ideas degenerate into conceptualized ideas.

Thus, even today Pythagoras is widely regarded as the inventor of mathematics in its modern sense. From the modern point of view, Pythagoras appears as a wondrous and strange visionary in whom authentic scientific genius was mingled with religious superstition and occultist charlatanry. He taught that number lay at the heart of reality, this being interpreted as a great pre-vision of the modern scientific view of the mathematical structure of the universe. However, modern mathematics is nothing more nor less than a superb system of concepts, as was persuasively argued by Alfred North Whitehead and Bertrand Russell in the early part of this century.

For Pythagoras, number was an idea, not a concept. It was a guide to self-inquiry and the transformed experience of being, rather than a principle for organizing the data of ordinary experience and articulating the analytic and combinatory functions of the intellect.

Understood in this light, modern mathematics results from the same historical dialectic as modern philosophy. Real ideas degenerate into conceptualized ideas. These conceptualized ideas are then, by the process of conceptual analysis, purged of that in them which is unverifiable by the ordinary mind. The teachings of

Pythagoras became the "philosophizing" of Pythagoreanism and, as such, fascinated the Western world throughout the centuries of late antiquity, bursting forth with renewed attraction in the Renaissance and eventually exerting a dominant influence on the fathers of modern science: Copernicus, Galileo, Kepler, and, above all, Isaac Newton. The early modern era abounds with Pythagorean philosophizing—perhaps even more so than in late antiquity. Formulations such as "the harmony of the spheres," "cosmic order," "the central sun," "force and counterforce," and many other Pythagorean/Hermetic expressions are altered into metaphysical concepts—conceptualized ideas—and galvanize some of the most influential minds of the era. They then are subjected to conceptual analysis by a Descartes, a Newton, a Leibniz and soon become the effective concepts of modern science—mathematics, physics, chemistry. Stripped of their apparently superstitious aspects, these Pythagorean ideas become the modern concepts of number, energy, and causal order, the great problem-solving mechanisms that have organized the whole of modern life through the development of scientific technology.

Thus, modern mathematics is nothing more or less than the criticism of Pythagoreanism. Mathematics, as we know it, has little to do with the primordial idea of number, as little as concepts have anything essential in common with ideas.

Here it is necessary to note something important about these apparently superstitious aspects of Pythagoreanism. Before coming under the scrutiny of conceptual analysis, Pythagorean formulation contained many elements which we nowadays would call mythical, symbolic, ritualistic, mystical, magical, and occult. Throughout the centuries Pythagoreanism has been associated with such things as magic squares, musical notations, mythological allusions, alchemical symbols, anatomical and physiological diagrams, and much else of this nature.

These elements may perhaps best be understood as disconnected remnants of what was once the full method of transmission of ideas by the school of Pythagoras. Of course, we do not know all the conditions which Pythagoras established for the transmission of his teaching. Historical documents tell us of his methodical use of parable and symbol, of meditation, of the discipline of silence, of the study of music and sacred dance, of the master-pupil relationship, and of specific degrees of initiation; we hear of indications concerning diet, sleep, sexual activity, and communal order; indications concerning family life, vocation, physical work; we hear of rituals involving certain distinct periods of the year and times of the day; there are rules of some distinct sort having to do with relationships among the brotherhood (which included women) and between members of the brotherhood and those outside it.

The "superstitious" elements are the only generally known surviving remnants of these methods and, of course, from such meager remnants it is impossible to reconstruct an adequate picture of the teaching of Pythagoras. I bring up this point about the superstitious elements of Pythagoreanism in order to clarify an interesting and significant historical fact about the immense influence of Pythagoreanism in the early modern era. At the same time that conceptual analysis was purging Pythagoreanism of its superstitious elements and laying the groundwork for the powerful conceptual system of modern science, the imagery connected with Pythagoreanism was widely adopted by visionary poets and artists throughout the European world. From Shakespeare to William Blake, from Goethe to Hölderlin, and perhaps including Dürer, Mozart, and the Florentine architect Brunelleschi, Pythagoreanism was the most important new source of artistic metaphor from the Renaissance onward.

Conceptual analysis rescued the problem-solving, explanatory aspects of Pythagoreanism; artistic feeling, on the other hand, appropriated the imaginative residue neglected by the scientific philosophers. Thus was created, in its modern form, the rupture between art and science corresponding in ourselves to the rupture between intellect and emotion, with all its disastrous consequences in our individual and collective lives.

It is a characteristic of philosophizing that it leaves an emotional residue when it is purged by conceptual criticism. The needs and longings that draw us to invent or believe in conceptualized ideas about God, immortality, or reality continue to exist in ourselves or in our culture even after the most thorough conceptual correction. The result is a condition of fragmentation or contradiction within the individual and within the culture. Within the individual, within ourselves, this condition of fragmentation can take many forms. In one part of my life, in one part of the psyche, I am analytic, critical, and scientific, carefully weighing and testing the coherence and utility of all general concepts; while in another part of my life and mind I am "religious," "spiritual," interested in art, morality, service to great causes. The need for contact with the higher lives on in these latter pursuits, but only at the emotional level. The contradiction between the intellectual and the emotional aspects of the self remains unresolved. Moreover, the condition of self-contradiction itself is veiled, buffered by opinions about oneself as being "a complex individual," "interestingly varied" in one's interests and concerns. This process of covering over the contradiction between the conceptual and valuational parts of the mind can go very far indeed—we shall consider it more fully in its proper place. For now, we can certainly find examples, if not in ourselves (it is almost impossible to see it in oneself), then in others—such as scientists who are simultaneously men of religious belief or moral fervor accepting doctrines or acting on assumptions about man and the universe that have little or no conceptual clarity or rational justification.

In the culture at large, this condition of fragmentation and internal contradiction also manifests itself in numerous ways, some obvious, some subtle. But in any case, terms like "pluralism," "tolerance," and "individualism" often mask what is simply lack of relationship between the parts of ourselves, while various superficial attempts to integrate the parts mask the absorption of one part by another—such as the secularization of religion under the banner of "relevance" and "social concern."

The formation of conceptualized ideas occurs when the ordinary intellect takes over the formulations of real ideas and converts them into concepts. When this happens, the part of the mind that longs for inner truth has already been left behind. Visionary critics of the contemporary era who seek to heal the present state of cultural and psychological fragmentation by harking back to premodern philosophizing or poetics have not seen this point. "Unity" of ordinary thought and ordinary emotion is precisely the enemy of truth. What is needed is the unity of pure thought and pure feeling. This authentic structural unity of human nature is, however, possible only with the development in man of an attention that can make contact with all the parts of the self. This attention first appears only when I myself am in question in the midst of life. The first function of real ideas is not to unite the parts of us into a superficial harmony, but to separate them—that is, to break down the deceptive unity called ego.

When we say that it is Pythagoras who stands behind Socrates, we are saying that there are ideas that bring us to authentic silence of the mind and support the initiatives of self-interrogation.

Clearly, the very word *philosophy*, which Pythagoras introduced, is such an idea. It identifies a part of the self that seeks something other than the satisfaction of material or psycho-social desires. In so doing, it encourages us to attend more carefully to those seemingly random and disconnected moments in life when a new feeling breaks through—the feeling of wonder or profound and impersonal doubt brought about through contact with immense forces of nature or the overwhelming disappointments and sufferings of human existence. Without such a guiding idea, these moments go by without being recognized for what they are: signs of another force of being within us calling to us.

It is this latent force within man which Pythagoras designated by the word *psyche*, soul. "Give attention to the soul" is a phrase that practically defines the whole of the teaching of Pythagoras and Socrates. Here the idea is that there is something within myself that corresponds to the highest principle of the universe, but which will not enter into my life automatically. A specific act of attention is required, that same attention which can appear, but only accidentally and in disconnected flashes, when the ordinary course of life is invaded by great disruption or when, without warning, a moment of silent feeling of new quality accompanies a single perception of something or someone. The idea of the soul was not expressed either by Pythagoras or by Socrates without the concomitant demand to cultivate that quality of attention, nor was it expressed without the help needed by a man to do that work. As has been said, the superstitions that surrounded imaginary Pythagoreanism were faint residues of that help.

The term *soul* became a conceptualized idea the moment this act of attention was misunderstood. "Give attention to the soul" becomes "tending the soul" only in the sense of forming concepts and images about oneself and entertaining fantastic opinions of man's automatic inner divinity, leading to exaggerated ethical programs and bitterly unrealizable moral demands. This is an aspect of philosophizing that deserves a separate name because of the unusually destructive influence it has had in the course of centuries. To speak of it as "psychologizing" or "moralizing" is equally appropriate, but perhaps the former term is better because these fantastic moral programs, when subjected to the purging scrutiny of conceptual analysis, become what we know as modern psychiatry.

It is not possible to run through, even briefly, all the ideas of Pythagoras. I will confine myself to mentioning several others that will be of special importance in the following chapters where we shall try to penetrate behind the problems of our contemporary life and culture.

Many of the ideas of Pythagoras long ago entered into our language in the form of words that we use every day without realizing their rich philosophical lineage. When we speak of the "world" or "cosmos" as an all-encompassing ordered whole, we are using a formulation introduced by Pythagoras. The critical point here is that the vast totality of the cosmos is knowable, intelligible. The cosmos "imitates number": that is, the whole order of the world obeys laws which can be known by the mind.

Stated in the above way, the idea of cosmos merely sounds like one of the clichés of the Western scientific attitude. But truth is not a cliché. If the idea sounds overfamiliar and obvious, it is only because we no longer feel what it means. We no longer feel what it means partly because the modern scientific concept of the cosmos has excised something essential from this formulation of Pythagoras.

The idea of cosmos is in no way comparable to the concept of universe. The cosmos is knowable in the sense that what is real and fundamental is purpose, intention, and harmony. Being is Mind. But it is not my mind; or, rather, it is the mind of man insofar as he develops all his mental, moral, and physical possibilities. The cosmos is knowable, but we cannot know it until we become similar to it. The modern concept of the universe retains only the first part of this statement—reality as knowable—but does away with the second part, the need for a development of the whole of man's psyche.

The idea of the cosmos and the concept of the universe both refer to all that we see and infer around us: biological life, the planet earth, the solar system, the sun, other suns and solar systems, all the galaxies—all the entities in the reaches of space which, as contemporary technology is now beginning to show, exhibit a completely unforeseen variety in size, structure, polarity, and tempo. All of this, together with the mathematical laws of physics, adds up to the universe in modern terms. But it is not cosmos, although it is contained by cosmos. In the Pythagorean idea there exist entities and substances permeating the universe we see, which have material, causal efficacy and power, but which are at the same time pure mind or approach very near to being pure mind. These "winds of heaven" or "etheric substances" are real and material, yet they are also nearly the same thing as number or law. They are more rational, more intelligible, more knowable than the things perceived through the senses, or through instruments, or through inferences made on the basis of conceptual mathematics and refined sensory perception. They are more knowable—that is, they are purer manifestations of mind.

For now, we shall have to leave the formulation at that—acknowledging the apparent paradox this idea contains for us: the paradox of a materiality existing at various levels of mind. We may, however, briefly note what became of this idea when it was conceptualized. In the conceptualized idea of the cosmos, mind and consciousness are separated off from matter. Two realms are posited: the realm of incorporeal being—nonmaterial reality—and the realm of material entities. The immaterial realm becomes conceptualized as a separately existing entity or entities. In religious philosophizing this becomes the concept of God and the angels. In metaphysical philosophizing, this notion of the immaterial realm becomes the conceptualized ideas of "the first cause," or "the noumenon," the "reality behind the appearances"—all understood as separately existing entities of some sort or other. Once the conceptualization is accepted, the door is open to a bewildering variety of pseudoexplanations of the perceived world with no possibility of verification, which is to say that the highest principles of reality are implicitly consigned to the realm of the unknowable. Something called "mysticism" is then invited in through the backdoor in order to bring these imaginary realities again into the realm of the knowable, the intelligible. Or else the mind of man is permanently judged to be incapable of knowing God or the First Cause, and finally permanently judged to be incapable of knowing anything beyond what is revealed to him in his ordinary state of consciousness. That which is inaccessible to the ordinary mind must be accepted on "faith." From here it is but a short step to the tyranny of "dogma" in its modern sense.

Out of this morass of conceptualized ideas about the cosmos there arose a "problem of philosophy" that even today occupies academicians and others. This is the so-called problem of *a priori* knowledge: Is certainty about the world attainable through thought alone or is all significant knowledge rooted in sensory experience? This problem has had a colossal influence in modern times, but it actually represents an advanced stage in the decay of the real idea of the cosmos. Certainly, according to Pythagoras, the cosmos, the deep order of nature, is knowable through self-knowledge—man is a microcosm. But this sort of self-knowledge involves a total inner inquiry into all aspects of the human structure as well as the arising within man of a conscious attention that can penetrate into the unconscious and harmonize all the disparate impulses within the human organism. So-called *a priori* knowledge, on the other hand—knowledge independent of sensory experience—bears only an imitative resemblance to this idea of self-knowledge. It is intellectual knowledge alone that is at issue in the problem of the *a priori*, rather than contemplative knowledge in its ancient sense. Intellectual knowledge alone—concepts alone—can do no more than organize the data provided by the instruments of perception. The ancient idea of knowing the cosmos through knowing oneself is based on the possibility of man's developing new powers of perception within himself. The issue in its modern form ignores or misunderstands that possibility.

Are the few ideas we have mentioned—number, the soul, the cosmos—enough to allow us, finally, to look with the eye of philosophy at the world we live in? Have we found our Socrates? Surely not. But we have to some extent *called* for him and what he represents: the effort of inquiry that seeks to penetrate behind the appearances of the world and of myself—the world as it presents itself in the form of menacing problems to be solved and our own apparent selves with all the seeming good and bad within us.

We have called for ideas, authentic ideas, to come to our aid. Will we be open to them? Or will we, too, spoil them in our haste to formulate answers? Behind the appearances lies the Question. Are we prepared to let the Question break through into our awareness, there to begin its long journey toward the heart?

In that spirit, I offer the following passage as a kind of invocation, written in the fourth century A.D. by the most famous biographer of Pythagoras, the Greek Iamblichus. The opening lines of this biography are as follows:

> Since it is usual with all men of sound understandings, to call on divinity, when entering on any philosophical discussion, it is certainly much more appropriate to do this in the consideration of that philosophy which justly receives its denomination from the divine Pythagoras. For as it derives its origin from the Gods, it cannot be apprehended without their inspiring aid. To which we may also add, that the beauty and magnitude of it so greatly surpasses human power, that it is impossible to survey it by a sudden view; but then alone can one gradually collect some portion of this philosophy, when, the Gods being his leaders, he quietly approaches to it. On all these accounts, therefore, having invoked the Gods as our leaders, and converting both ourselves and our discussion to them, we shall acquiesce in whatever they may command us to do.[*]

To this we may simply add that in the teaching of Pythagoras, the gods are the ideas and ideas are gods.

[*]*Iamblichus' Life of Pythagoras*, trans. Thomas Taylor (London: John Watkins, 1965), p. 1.

PART II

Wendy, Sim, and Other Philosophers

CHAPTER 4

Nondepartmental Offering

Two years ago I received an invitation from the headmaster of a private school not far from where I live. Would I be willing to speak to a class of high-school students about philosophy? Distinguished guests from the local community were being asked to conduct small classes throughout the day. Students would choose from a smorgasbord of civic leaders, scientists, artists and craftsmen, journalists, and college teachers such as myself.

The fact that my own children attended the school made it difficult for me to say no, which I would have done ordinarily. Speak to young teenagers about philosophy? The thought terrified me. Twenty years of teaching college-age students had made me painfully aware of how difficult it is to discuss serious ideas in a way that does justice to both the academic needs of younger people and the deeper wish for understanding that brings them to philosophy in the first place. How many times had I come to the end of a lecture or a whole course feeling I had closed more doors than I had opened? Well, with my university students, most of whom were in their twenties, I could always excuse myself a little. By the time they appeared in the university they had already "shut down" to the same extent as the rest of us. God forbid that I should ever try to play the guru. In any case, at the very least I could help them experience the value of conceptual analysis and intellectual criticism. If, while questioning their own assumptions and beliefs, some of them could then glimpse the power of the great ideas we were studying, then perhaps I had done all that a professor of philosophy could and should do. Perhaps.

But teenagers? I remembered a little of what I was like at that age. I had most definitely not "shut down." I believed in Truth and I believed in Answers. I needed to serve something higher than myself and yet, at the same time, I yearned to establish my own personal ego.

There was one experience of a certain kind that only much later in my life did I understand. I remember it down to the smallest detail. I had just turned fourteen. It was a bright October afternoon and I was walking home from school. I remember the trees and the colored leaves underfoot. My thoughts were wandering when suddenly my name, "Jerry," said itself in my mind. I stopped in my tracks. I whispered to myself: "I am." It was astonishing. "I exist." I began to walk again, but very slowly. And my existence was walking with me, inside me. I am fourteen years old and I am.

And that is all. I did not speak about this experience to anyone, and for no other reason than that I gradually forgot about it. I went on reading every kind of book about the mind, nature, science; about philosophy; I read great novels. I plunged into classical music. But not once did anything I read, nor anyone or anything I heard, make mention, even remotely, of such an experience. Nothing in my environment or education reminded me of it. How could that be? What is culture, what is education, if it makes no place for that? And further, what is the right way of supporting that experience without spoiling it even more by the wrong kind of talk?

There were other far less lofty reasons to be afraid of speaking about philosophy to teenagers. I knew, again from personal experience, what a keen eye for pretense I had at the age of fifteen. Let this or that teacher, no matter how sincerely he tried to impart something of value, exhibit the slightest trace of pomposity or self-righteousness, and he was finished. Our circle of friends would afterwards gather together and unceremoniously consign him for all time to our private cage wherein resided the butt of all our jokes: various teachers of "great literature," "personal hygiene," "moral values," and so forth. He would never be taken seriously again.

I was sure I would have to give up all my professional tricks. Without these tricks—such as covering over ignorance by erudite references to other texts, or masking one's own confusion by calling some point or other "extremely complex" or "very advanced," or throwing a difficult query back to the poor student (for "pedagogical" purposes) while one ransacked one's brain for a respectable answer—without these tricks, how would I fare? I had been fond of referring to philosophy as an awakener of the real, gut-level questions of life, and equally fond of complaining that students were not free to address these questions in present-day educational institutions. But what if someone actually asked one of these questions? Was I really prepared for that?

On the morning of my talk I was as nervous as I had been when I first started teaching twenty years before. There they were, about fifteen good-looking boys and girls, and there I was—talking, talking, talking. I couldn't stop talking. Hands started waving in the air and I finally recognized one of the students. But no sooner did she start to bring her question out than I steamrolled over it with an answer that left her absolutely no room for further questioning. I went on talking—engagingly, amusingly, animatedly, bringing in Plato's cave here, the Upanishads there, St. Augustine's concept of evil, Kierkegaard, Spinoza, Hegel . . .

Time flew by. The bell rang and, suddenly, the class was over. That was it, that was all. As the students cheerfully filed past me and as I smiled at each of them, exchanging a few informal remarks, I began to realize in my guts what had happened. To be precise: *nothing*. Nothing had happened.

I remained behind in the empty classroom, seated behind the

desk. A dense fog began to lift and images of young, open faces appeared before me. Then another bell rang and I heard a soft tapping at the glass door. The next class was due to start. The students had been waiting politely and, no doubt wonderingly, for me to come out of the room.

In the days that followed, each time I thought of that fiasco it stopped me in my tracks. Gradually, but distinctly, I began to recognize by its "taste" a certain process taking place with respect to my own cherished views about philosophy and the education of young people. I myself was coming into question; I hadn't expected that. One never does.

And now I am in New York breakfasting with an old friend who has become the director of an interesting new philanthropic foundation. Am I planning any projects, he asks me, for which I would like to apply for support?

Immediately, the image of my one experience with high-school students rises in front of me and, to my astonishment, I find myself saying, with complete assurance in my voice: "What I'd really like to try is to teach a course in philosophy to teenagers."

Who was it who said, "Be careful what you ask for in life—you may get it"? Now, as I write, it is the end of August, 1980. In two weeks I begin my course at San Francisco University High School. The announcement bravely reads as follows:

Nondepartmental Offering

THE CRISIS OF THE MODERN WORLD

Beyond the massive problems of the modern era—problems of natural resources, war, crime, the family, social justice—there lies a deep confusion about the meaning of human life itself. Who am I? Why was I born? What is the purpose of human life on earth? These questions have been asked since the beginning of time, but never have the answers been harder to find than now and here at the end of the twentieth century. The aim of this course is to connect the problems of the day with the questions of the ages. This is a course in philosophy, the art of looking for the real world behind the appearances.

Issues to be treated may include:

—the new religious movements;

—the cosmos: a great machine or a living organism?

—work as a human activity;

—good technology and bad technology;

—the problem and mystery of death.

Readings will be drawn from sources both ancient and modern, Eastern and Western. The aim of the course is to do philosophy, not just to learn about it.

All summer long, I have been trying to plan this course. In my formal grant application I had written about the need to provide such material to young people of high-school age:

> The same need, of course, exists in students who sign up for philosophy classes at the university level throughout the country. Like so many people in the contemporary culture, they are all seeking ideas that can actually guide the conduct of life and the search for meaning. But, for the most part, students end their school years disappointed and more confused than ever about values—easy prey for any ideology, guru, or stimulant that comes off the streets promising to satisfy their craving for a connection to something bigger than themselves. What is particularly disturbing to me is the fact that so many students entering college have already had their most precious intellectual power—the sense of wonder—crushed or distorted.

It is one thing to speak about this need, however, and it is quite another to know how to answer it. I have been asking everyone for advice. Everyone, without exception, enthusiastically approves of the whole idea of such a course. "Long overdue," says one experienced educator, his eyes lighting up. A psychologist who works with young people burnt out by drugs or cults considers it "a most important step." "Now," he says, "I can tell anxious parent groups that something is being tried somewhere." He throws back at me my own words about our educational system's turning out a nation of "religious illiterates," and quotes something I once wrote likening the present situation with the previous generation's tabu against speaking about sex. He agrees with the comparison and endorses the offering of a sort of program in "metaphysical hygiene" for young people. But when I ask him how he would prevent such a program from becoming as ineffectual and dreary as the hygiene classes of our own youth, he has nothing to say. He merely jokes that whereas he had to learn about sex in the streets, today's kids have to learn about Being in the streets.

Very well, no one knows what to do; I can accept that. So I have tried asking people about their own adolescence: What was the most important book for them when they were young? What turned them on to serious ideas? I ask them that because I have been scrutinizing every book in my library trying to find at least the right readings to start with. But every book or author mentioned is one I have already considered and rejected. Spinoza? Too difficult. Hermann Hesse? Too sentimental. Plato? Of course, but not to begin with; they will have heard too much about him from other sources. Grimm's fairy tales? Rich with real ideas, but teenagers are still too close to childhood to approach them freely. Nietzsche? Camus? Too subjective. Kierkegaard? Too subtle— and also, although anyone with a search can see he is as far as possible from being conventionally "religious," young people would be too distracted by the Christian language of Kierkegaard; one can't begin with Kierkegaard. The Stoics—Epictetus and Marcus Aurelius? No, although I myself had been deeply moved by them when quite young. Examining Epictetus again two months ago, I was disappointed by the moralizing tone that the Victorian translations had put into his writings. Moralizing in any form is the kiss of death in pondering great ideas.

So I have thought again of how I first became interested in ideas when I was young. What author first helped me? The answer surprises me: Bertrand Russell.

Had anyone advised me to start my class with Russell, I would have dismissed the suggestion out of hand. I had not even considered his work over the summer—Bertrand Russell, lucid, witty, skeptical, a principal founder of modern logical analysis who approached the great questions of philosophy with little more than a very sharp pencil in his hand; Russell, who brought into the twentieth century the faith of the Enlightenment in scientific method as the model of understanding; who could dispose of Plato in a paragraph, or the whole of the religious traditions of mankind in a brief and amusing chapter. No, not Russell.

Then how to explain the immense impact that his writings had on me when I was sixteen? Although he cleverly tears at every ancient and medieval metaphysical doctrine, I did not feel clever or even wish to be clever after reading him. Although he demonstrates the logical flaws in the Western idea of God, he did not shake my belief in the existence of a Creator—on the contrary. Master of the modern scientific canons of knowledge, he pictures man as a wisp of consciousness in an immense, indifferent universe that will inevitably snuff out his life and the very memory of his life on earth. Then why did I keep turning to his books for the very thing I would wish to bring to my own students—a sense of man's enduring place in a greater scale of reality?

I remember to the day and hour the first time I read Russell. It was shortly after the start of my third year in high school. I had just earned my driver's license and on Sunday mornings I used to take the family car and drive out of the city in order to be by myself in some wooded area. On the seat next to me was a pile of books representing the week's foraging in the public library. I remember that at that time I was very taken with the novels of Thomas Hardy; their austere representation of the human condition confirmed, in some sweet way, my own loneliness. This time, among the books beside me was one I had picked off the library shelf without thinking too much about it: *Human Knowledge: Its Scope and Limits* by Bertrand Russell.

I mentioned loneliness, but I don't mean to imply anything beyond what many, if not most, adolescents experience in our culture as a result, I believe, of their not being sufficiently occupied. This problem takes on a colossally destructive dimension, however, when it exists within the confusion that has now spread everywhere about the nature and function of the family. To my mind, the question exists in the following form. The family is the matrix of the growth of feeling in man. Modern psychological theories of the family have concentrated mainly on the emotions of loving acceptance and personal warmth. Traditionalists stress its function of inculcating moral values and a sense of responsibility. Others speak of preparing the child "for life," and there are countless other theories as well as numerous experiments being tried throughout the modern world with different forms of the family. But something seems to me to be left out in all these views of the role of the family, and this something has to do with the true range of feeling that is possible for man and necessary for his complete development. Father and mother: Sooner or later in every individual life something must take their place, something that is not external. In a grown-up man, what is the source of aspiration and love of self? What guides one's own individual struggle for Being in a grown-up man? From what place in oneself comes authentic shame and authentic pride? And to what, and with what quality, are the impulses of reverence and honor directed in a grown-up man? These are not rhetorical questions and I hope I will not be misunderstood if I tentatively propose an answer: As a child loves father and mother, so the man may come to love truth.

That particular Sunday was especially dreary for me. The Sunday boredom had set in even before noon. By the time I parked the car near an especially beautiful stretch of the Wissahickon

Creek north of Philadelphia, I was encased in self-pity. On the way, I had tuned the radio to whatever music would support this emotional state, and now I regarded all the beauty around me through its lens. Anything to intensify it, anything to bring emotion of any kind. It was the only way I could feel alive. Surely, that is the fundamental meaning of the boredom that begins to be such a dominant fact of life when we are young: the yearning for emotion. Out of this yearning come many things—including some forms of crime.

I picked up a book and began to read—it was Hardy's *Jude the Obscure*, perfect for the mood I was in. But right beneath it was the Russell book, and the title, *Human Knowledge*, drew me. While enjoying the crushing sorrows of poor Jude, my mind kept wandering to the title of Russell's book. I soon put down Hardy and took up Russell.

I stayed glued to that book for the next three hours without even thinking of lunch. Why? What happened?

I wasn't able to follow much of Russell's sophisticated thought about science and human experience. So there was no question of this teenager agreeing or disagreeing with his point of view. Something much more important and elemental was taking place in me. Russell spoke about human language and I realized that language exists—I spoke language, I read language; poetry and novels and books, and perhaps music and art were also language. He discussed space and time, and I realized that space is all around me, that everything exists in space; and time flows everywhere, I am in it, everything is in it—but what is it? And there is ethics; my worries and problems—were they not *ethics?* And there is mind—I have mind and I have a body, and everything I see is a body, but where is the mind? My loneliness dissolved; it simply dried up as the various aspects of myself were presented to me as objects of inquiry in the large world. I knew then that there exists something that one might call *clarity*. I knew it as a feeling, a wish. It was an entirely new feeling and yet, at the same time, strangely intimate and warm. Critics of the contemporary era often speak of the sense of alienation and cosmic loneliness produced by the modern emphasis on the scientific attitude. They have their point, but it has no weight when placed against the first taste of objectivity toward oneself. There is nothing cold about it. On the contrary, then and only then did I first begin to feel that there is a home for man behind the appearances of this happy/unhappy world. I could not read many more novels after that in my adolescence. I never even finished *Jude the Obscure*.

So now I look upon this summer's efforts to prepare my course as somewhat beside the point. I have been worrying too much about the content of the course and not enough about the search that needs to be brought to all philosophy, no matter what its content. I don't agree with Russell; I believe his vision of reality is shallow, his concepts of human nature and knowledge lead nowhere. Yet his is a greater mind than my own, and I once needed to listen to it.

Today is September 10 and in two hours I meet with my young class for the first time. I feel that I am back at square one. Yet, for some reason, I am not nervous about it anymore.

CHAPTER 5

Questions
in the Margin

There are fifteen students in the class, exactly the right number. But before and after the class, I found myself wondering more about the students passing me in the hall who hadn't signed up for the course. At their age, would I have risked taking such a course? Maybe not. There was one boy who particularly interested me and I watched him for a few minutes. He was sitting by his locker amid a disorderly stack of textbooks and notebooks spread out on the floor. His head was buried in his new physics text and he was rapidly turning the pages, completely oblivious to what was going on around him. I went up to him.

"Can you tell me where room eleven is?" I said.

He looked up, startled. He could have been me; he had a round face, small features, and unkempt brown hair; his shirt hung out on one side of his trousers. "It's right over there, Professor," he said, pointing just down the corridor. So he knew who I was.

"Taking physics this term?" I said.

His eyes lit up. "Yes, Professor. I want to go into science. I wanted to take your course, but it's at the same time as physics."

It *was* me. I walked down the corridor, smiling about that boy. He had said, "I want to go into science," in the way an older person would have said, "I want to know, I want to understand."

But when he grew up would he recognize that his wish to under-stand was as much a part of his nature as his arms and legs or the color of his eyes? I am convinced that man is born with that wish implanted in the very tissues of his body. Why and when does it stop sounding in so many of us? Is it possible to insert even one or two ideas in young people's minds that can come to their aid when life begins to do its job on them, to help them remember that wish or be moved by it, even unconsciously, toward a real search for truth?

I met my class, talked briefly about the meaning of the word "philosophy." They were far more nervous than I was. The assistant headmaster had told me that some of the brightest students in the school had signed up for the class; that partly explained their tension. Even one real idea, presented in a diffuse and simplified manner, can be a bit frightening to a mind accustomed to master-ing concepts.

I began by asking them to write down the one question they would put if they were to meet someone really wise—a Moses or a Socrates or a Buddha. What came back were cramped little fragments written in the margins of the paper or surrounded by immense white spaces:

"Is God real?"

"Why are we here?"

"Must there be a reason?"

"Where's it all going—the universe?"

"Why was man given a more advanced brain than other ani-mals?"

I tucked the papers into my folder, promising to discuss all these questions as the course proceeded. But to myself I was mak-ing quite another promise. I would give them the same task in a month or so. By then they would not find it so strange to have to formulate "the question in the heart." Not that they would find it easier—on the contrary. I promised myself they would be thinking about their question in almost every activity of their lives: in other classes, at the movies or in front of the TV, at sports, at dinner with their families, out on a date, or at a party—and even, for a few of them probably, before lighting up a joint. I promised myself that in a month or so they would be, if only a little, "poisoned" by philosophy. Our culture, our society has no place where the ultimate questions are honored as questions. Every institution and social form we have is devoted either to solving problems or providing pleasure; the school, the family, the church, medicine, entertainment, job—even funerals are designed to comfort us rather than keep us in front of the question that the death of a loved one practically screams out at us: *You, too, will die—why have you lived?* Our questions, too, are like stunted cries written on a separate sheet of blank paper.

September 18

We are meeting three times a week for forty-five minutes at the tail end of the school day. I like that arrangement. They are tired by then and a little fidgety, but this is outweighed by the fact that our class is the impression they leave school with and take home with them. Even being tired is not so bad. Let them spend their mental attention on geometry or French or chemistry where it really is needed; let them come to philosophy a little less interested in figuring things out. I don't mind that a bit. Because if under those conditions they become interested, maybe it comes from a different place in them. I want them to be dreaming at night about philosophy.

As I expected, what really touches them are metaphysical and cosmological ideas. As an experiment, I started each class this week by discussing a problem of current concern: the ecological crisis, the threat of nuclear war, and the problem of world poverty. I only wish I had a filmed record of their reactions to show the difference between the beginning and the end of each class. In the beginning, out came all their opinions and moral concerns—

everyone talking at once, hands waving in the air, arguments, information from the latest newspaper article or TV show. Some of them are actually extremely well-informed. We all played our parts, as though reading from a script entitled "Interesting Exchange About a Serious Issue." Because they are a little tired, however, and because they are not quite adults yet, it is easy to see that their opinions have not yet become fully crystallized in them. In one moment they are passionately denouncing some ecological crime and in the next moment they are giggling or just staring out the window.

God bless them. And God bless this condition of uncrystallized opinion which our society blindly condemns and seeks to eradicate by every means possible. I related to them a half-amusing experience of mine just around this point.

It was in 1968 when I was a visiting lecturer at Columbia University in New York. That was the time of the great student riots and Columbia was one of the schools where it all began. Buildings were being occupied, chaos and the threat of violence reigned everywhere. I was coming out of Butler Library one November morning when suddenly from out of nowhere a microphone appeared in front of my face. At the other end was a flushed and eager TV reporter. Like birds flocking to a crust of bread, about a half-dozen other news people also ran up to me, one of them holding a portable video camera and others with notebooks and pencils poised in their hands.

"Do you teach here, sir?" asked the man holding the microphone.

I nodded yes in a sort of daze.

"Which side do you think is right?" he asked, and positioned the microphone so close to my mouth that for a moment I thought he was going to push it inside my mouth.

I moved my head back a little. "I don't know," I said.

He stared at me blankly, and then rephrased his question.

"Do you think the students are justified in the actions they have taken today?" Back came the microphone. I saw the camera inching in a little closer.

"I don't know," I said again. It was true. I really didn't know who was right. In that moment I saw something arising out of the reporters and from within myself that I was to see again and again both here at Columbia and later back at San Francisco State during the student strikes that captured so much of the world's attention. One of the chief features of any period of mass agitation is the immense pressure to take a position; and not only to take a position, but to believe in it passionately down to the marrow of one's bones. This is called "morality," or "commitment." But often it is nothing other than fear.

The reporter continued to stare at me uncomprehendingly. Then, suddenly, the expression on his face changed. Never in my life has anyone looked at me with such revulsion and contempt. "You mean," he said, and the words came out with great difficulty, "you have . . . *no opinion?*" He could as well have accused me of mass murder.

Whenever I tell this story to others, I usually embroider the facts to make it more amusing than it really was and to make myself look better. I have myself replying, "Don't knock it! It has taken me years to reach the point where I can have no opinion on something like this!" But actually I only shook my head while watching the reporters backing away from me as though they had just discovered I had some loathsome and very contagious disease.

My telling the story did little to stem the flow of opinions coming from the class. But as soon as cosmological or metaphysical ideas were introduced into the discussion it was as though a magic wand had been waved over the class. Fidgeting stopped. Wisecracking stopped. Interrupting and talking out at the same time stopped. An attention that was quiet, open, and unforced appeared in the room.

For example, ecology. How to preserve man's biological environment in a world addicted to its accelerated destruction? Nations and people have to change their life-styles, said one student. Another argued for the development of "intermediate technology" (she had been reading Schumacher). The subject of whales and rain forests led one student to propose a sort of international task force and pressure group. This led to the idea of world government, which one student claimed was unrealistic. He was shouted down by others who argued that since it was now a matter of physical survival on the planet, the governments of the world could come together out of sheer self-interest. Yet another student who had been studying the American Indian spoke of "walking lightly on the earth." This brought the whole discussion back to the problem of man's relationship to nature.

At just that point I asked one of those questions which, for very understandable reasons, have become a sort of joke among sophisticated people but which, under certain circumstances, acquire the primordial power that they once had for almost all of us. During a brief lull in the noisy exchange, I said:

"What is man?"

Silence ensued. After a few seconds, I added:

"And why is he on this earth?"

October 1

I must find a way to get acquainted with these students individually. I announced today that if anyone wanted to speak to me, I would remain after class or I would make a private appointment with them. But no one stayed and no one asked to see me. I thought at first it was only because of the material we had just discussed. The war between Iran and Iraq had just started and I had asked them to read an interesting essay about war by Samuel Dresner, a rabbi who puts forth a very different view of man's place in the cosmic scheme than any of the students had ever heard in their churches or synagogues. A very different and a rather chilling view. Citing certain rabbinic commentaries (Breshit

Rabbah 8), and echoing several little-known doctrines that may be found in the writings of the Kabbalists, Dresner speaks of the creation of man as no more nor less than a great experiment by God. The imminence of atomic war, argues Dresner, portends that the human experiment may be about to end in failure, a consequence of man's inability or unwillingness to occupy his intended place on this planet. He writes:

> Man's continued existence is by no means guaranteed.
> . . . There is no stability or certainty to man's existence.
> The angels opposed the creation of man; the forces of truth
> and justice opposed the creation of man. The creation of
> man was opposed because the evil that would come forth
> from him was foreseen. The creation of man was opposed
> because man's power to hurt, his will to destroy, was fore-
> seen. Notwithstanding, God created man (according to the
> rabbis) in the hope that the good would conquer the evil,
> the power to love would conquer the power to hurt, and
> the will to obey His will would conquer the will to destroy.
> The history of man, however, has been the history of God's
> disappointment with man.*

Dresner then cites the numerous places in the Old Testament (Adam, Cain, Noah and many others) where "the Almighty was about to end the human experiment." God created and destroyed many worlds before He created ours. Now, says Dresner, "perhaps our Earth [is about to] take its place among the others which God is said to have created and destroyed."

> What the prophets feared most was God's abandon-
> ment of man, the silencing of His voice, the withdrawal of

---

*Samuel H. Dresner, "Man, God and Atomic War," *God and the H-Bomb*, ed. Donald Keys (New York; 1961, Bernard Geis Associates, 1961). p.130.

His presence. . . . Perhaps this is the meaning of our time.
If man wants to destroy himself, God seems to say, "Let
him. I have had enough. I shall try again elsewhere."*

I was certainly not oblivious to the effect this idea had on the
students. Coming as it did after a week's discussion of man's place
in the scheme of nature, it was being taken far more in the spirit
of a scientific hypothesis than as some conventionally religious
pronouncement of doom.

Therefore it entered right into them as something to be taken
seriously.

However, even I was surprised by the degree of thoughtfulness
it engendered. Questions about ethics and morality arose, but with
quite a different cast than is usually the case. If I were to put it
abstractly, I would say that what deepened their questions about
ethical issues was that they saw such questions in a cosmological
perspective, as questions of what man *is* rather than what he must
do. The agitation usually associated with moral dilemmas receded
in front of the sense of a greater scale of reality in which man's
place, man's *being*, is at issue.

In order to test this perception of mine, I ended the class by
raising one of those philosophical problems most argued about
when the subject of war comes up: Is taking another life ever
justified? Usually, this sort of issue is guaranteed to generate con-
troversy—killing is wrong, but one has the right to self-defense,
etc. Killing is wrong, but one must protect one's family, etc.
Killing is wrong, but there are such things as just wars, for example, the war against Nazi Germany, etc. Such discussions also
invariably end with the conclusion that some form of world government is needed. And everyone goes home happy, even though
suspecting down deep that nothing of the sort is ever going to take
place among the nations of the world. Everyone goes home half-

*Ibid., p. 132.

consciously aware that carefully defined distinctions between murder and socially justified killing are irrelevant to the question that
lies behind the problem of war, the question of the real origins
and meaning of violence.

"How can anyone ever decide whether killing is right or wrong?"
said one student.

"What do you mean?" I said.

He didn't answer. "I know what he means," said another student, after an uncomfortable pause. All eyes turned to this girl,
Lois, who hardly ever spoke in class.

"He means that if you hate someone you can't help yourself.
You just want to kill them."

"That's right!" said the first student, whose name was Sim
(short for Simon).

Lois was a tall, fair-complexioned girl with soft blue eyes and
fluffy blond braids. Her face was perfectly round. Although she
rarely spoke, she paid very close attention to everything; her eyes
were always open wide, her lips always parted in an expression of
mild astonishment.

"How can you tell people not to hate other people?" she said.
"Birds fly, fish swim, people hate."

"That's right," Sim said again. He was short, compactly built
with high cheekbones and a slight narrowing at the corners of his
eyes that gave his face a suggestion of Asiatic impassiveness. This
in sharp contrast to the eagerness with which he plunged into every
idea. "But people also love, too, don't they?" he said, directing his
statement at Lois. Then he turned to me and asked:

"What makes people hate or love?"

A hand shot up in the middle of the class, but Sim wanted me
to answer. However, as I was about to say something, he cast his
eyes down and gave out a long, low whistle. "You know what?"
he said. "Are all the wars of human history just that—love and
hate? Think about it!" He whistled again in amazement. "Millions
and billions of people, bombs, terror, destruction, masses of peo-

ple moving from place to place—Jesus! Is it all just emotions? The
planet earth is floating in emotions!" Lights started going on in
Sim's eyes.

On this note the class came to an end. I sat at my desk pretending to be gathering up papers, waiting to see who would want
to speak privately to me. But everyone slowly filed out.

When I went into the corridor I saw Sim with his back to me
talking to two girls not from our class. The girls were giggling
about something Sim was saying. I decided to walk past them. I
glanced at Sim as I went by and was shocked to see what was in
his face as our eyes met in greeting. It was fear. This disturbed me
very much.

Of course, the last thing I wanted was the sort of pal-sy friend-
liness that would reduce philosophical ideas to intriguing puzzles.
A certain *kind* of fear was quite all right—the fear that is actually
a glimpse of the scale of great ideas, a man's first movement toward
allowing ideas into the heart. This sort of fear, which is more
accurately termed awe, can eventually become that feeling toward
the higher which is an indispensable impulse on the way to self-
knowledge, and which has been named "the fear of God" in the
great traditional teachings. In this direction lies the experience of
authentic remorse of conscience, the most powerful transforming
force in the life of man.

But the fear in Sim's eyes as I walked past him was nothing
even remotely related to any of that. It was guilt, as though somehow great truths demanded he not dally with pretty girls or something. My God, was I unwittingly making ideas into policemen in
the same way our whole culture has twisted the teachings of Moses
and Christ?

This possibility gnawed at me for the rest of the day. I wanted
the sense of demand to come from the ideas themselves, not from
some authority figure or from some system of moralistic regula-
tions. Our discussion of cosmological ideas had provided an immense scale of reality within which to think quietly and seriously

about man's place in nature—the place he now occupied and the place he is meant to occupy. The subject of war and violence had then emerged as a poignant question within that greater scale of universal ideas. The existence of war was an index of mankind's low level of being. Behind the problem of war lay the question of the place of emotion in the structure of human nature, and not only that, but also the place of emotion in the whole scheme of nature. This is a very powerful question. There is war, the problem of war. There is the yearning among all peoples for a solution to this engulfing problem; now, of course, more than at any other time in history. And there are all the proposed theories about the causes of war.

Between the problem of war and the numerous solutions proposed throughout history—the systems of morals, the ideologies, the religious and political blueprints—between the problem and the "solutions" there rises up the Question: What are the emotions of man? What sort of force or energy do they represent in the whole balance of life on earth? It is a cosmic, metaphysical question that goes beyond the usual categories by which we classify and perceive the world around us. The emotions, the negative emotions by which man lives and moves, are part of the atmosphere of earth. Under their influence, as Sim began to express it, planetary changes take place as much as under the influence of climate, or the shifting of continents. These are the lights that started to turn on in Sim's mind, I saw that. It is a cosmic question that cuts into the heart like a knife—because it is also a question about myself, as impersonal and intimate as every great question of philosophy must be.

Yet here was Sim averting his eyes from me as though I were some damned priest . . . or . . . schoolteacher!

October 8

Still no one has taken any sort of initiative, but I have decided on a simple method of getting to speak privately with them without making it obvious why. God forbid they should suspect that I am interested only in observing the arising in them of the wish for truth, their own wish, unforced and without pretense. I want them, of course, to feel that I am interested in them as individuals, but I want them to wonder why.

I have put about a dozen books on reserve in the school library and am requiring each of the students to choose one of these books and write a report about it. I told them I would have to meet with each of them separately in order to judge which book would be best for them, but that meanwhile they should look over all of them. From the way they responded to this assignment, I can tell that some of them are already beginning to smell a rat. Good. They all feel the demand to produce something—that is, they are relieved to see some structure emerging in the course. But some of them are now vaguely aware that the real aim has nothing to do with accomplishing anything. My task is to engage the part of them that needs to achieve while calling gently to the part that dreams of Truth. In the first half of my task I will have to be credible, believable—but not too much. In the second half, I will have to be subtle, indirect—but again, not too much so.

I, who am myself so rarely in contact with these two aspects of my own nature, how can I presume to guide another in this realm? I brush aside these doubts. In the first place, there is no question here of guiding anyone. I myself am looking, seeking. Can I detect the difference in these young people between the love of wisdom and the need to function happily in the world around them? To see this difference in them, I must try to see it in myself as well. I discover again and again that the real questions of living, that which lies behind the world of appearances and problems, emerge out of this one indestructible Question of my own two natures.

I keep thinking of those crabbed little formulations scrawled on blank sheets of paper the first day of class. In another year or two even that would no longer be possible for most of them. For most of us, our questions are educated out of us by the time we reach so-called maturity. I want them to feel *permitted* to ask great questions. Not to act a part, not to pretend—although even that is not altogether bad. But it is far better to feel the natural right to ask of the universe those simple, gut-level questions that are strongest in childhood, or which appear in moments of great disappointment or tragedy. One hears everywhere of rights—the right to life, the right to choose, to do what one wants with one's body, etc. But there is a deeper right within human nature: the right to ask, Who am I? Why am I here? Are there great Answers to these questions? Of course there are. But they do not appear until one has learned how to ask with the whole of oneself.

A good friend of mine, who understands what I am trying, says I am inculcating faith. I can accept that. It is not, however, faith in something—God forbid it. It is simply faith itself, without any object, without any awareness even, or self-consciousness. Faith I define as the deeply sensed permission to seek meaning. Amid all the beliefs of our era, belief in religion (rather than God), belief in science (rather than truth), belief in morality (rather than goodness), what has been stifled and crushed is faith that emanates from the essence of man. Down deep, we have been forbidden by fear and vanity to ask the questions of the heart. Thus we grow up settling for the answers of the personality.

Kierkegaard has correctly diagnosed the illness of contemporary man as fear without an object—which he called dread. The way out, I think, is the nourishing of faith without an object—which we may call the search.

Which books to place on the shelf? This is no great difficulty, now that I know my aim.

CHAPTER 6

A Strange Warmth

I have placed the following books on reserve:

The *Dialogues of Plato* (Jowett translation)
The Bhagavad Gita (Mascaro translation)
Will Durant, *The Story of Philosophy*
C. S. Lewis, *The Screwtape Letters*
David Hume, *Dialogues on Natural Religion*
Carlos Castaneda, *The Teachings of Don Juan*
Isha Schwaller de Lubicz, *Her-Bak* (Vol. I)
René Daumal, *Mount Analogue*
Janwillem van de Wetering, *The Empty Mirror*
Lizelle Reymond, *My Life with a Brahmin Family*
Bertrand Russell, *Human Knowledge*
John G. Neihardt, *Black Elk Speaks*

I have had my first appointment: Wendy Behrens. As luck would have it, the class discussion that day opened up an aspect of this whole project that I needed to be alone with before proceeding further in any direction. But I did not want to cancel my appointment and defer the chance to get to know one of the students. As it turned out, my meeting with Wendy helped me to understand something of critical importance about what I was trying.

During the class, I was lecturing about Buddhism and getting nowhere. The subject of Buddhism had come up in our attempt to discuss the problem of work and vocation, a topic of great interest and concern to everyone in the class. What is meaningful work? Must labor or a job always be a burden? I had assigned them a chapter from E. F. Schumacher's *Small Is Beautiful*, where he examines this issue in light of the Buddhist doctrine of "right livelihood." He writes:

> The modern economist has been brought up to consider "labor" or work as little more than a necessary evil. From the point of view of the employer, it is in any case simply an item of cost, to be reduced to a minimum if it cannot be eliminated altogether, say, by automation. From the point of view of the workman, it is a "disutility"; to work is to make a sacrifice of one's leisure and comfort, and wages are a kind of compensation for the sacrifice. Hence the ideal from the point of view of the employer is to have output without employees, and the ideal from the point of view of the employee is to have income with employment.*

Buddhism, by contrast:

> . . . takes the function of work to be at least threefold: to give a man a chance to utilize and develop his faculties; to enable him to overcome his egocenteredness by joining with other people in a common task; and to bring forth the goods and services needed for a becoming existence.**

The consequences of this view, according to Schumacher, are endless. The Buddhist would consider it little short of criminal "to organize work in such a manner that it becomes meaningless,

---

*E. F. Schumacher, *Small Is Beautiful* (New York: Harper & Row, 1973), p. 51.
**Ibid., pp. 51–52.

boring, stultifying, or nerve-racking for the worker." It would indicate:

> . . . an evil lack of compassion and a soul-destroying de-
> gree of attachment to the most primitive side of this worldly
> existence. Equally, to strive for leisure as an alternative to
> work would be a complete misunderstanding of one of the
> basic truths of human existence, namely that work and
> leisure are complementary parts of the same living process
> and cannot be separated without destroying the joy of work
> and the bliss of leisure.*

Finally, by way of summation, Schumacher writes:

> While the materialist is mainly interested in goods, the
> Buddhist is mainly interested in liberation. But Buddhism
> is "The Middle Way" and therefore in no way antagonistic
> to physical well-being. It is not wealth that stands in the
> way of liberation but the attachment to wealth; not the
> enjoyment of pleasurable things but the craving for them.**

All of this, in any case, provided me with a good pretext for
speaking about the Buddhist concept of the self. But no matter
how I twisted and turned, no matter what I said, the class seemed
completely unmoved by the idea that man's usual sense of self-
identity is no more than a three-dimensional mirage.

While trying one approach after another, however, I experienced a little internal event that put my efforts in a new light.
A straight-A student named Eric Koppleman had asked a good,
rational question about the parallel between Plato's notion of
opinion and the Buddhist teaching about ignorance. They

*Ibid., p. 52.
**Ibid., p. 54.

seemed similar to him. He was right; they are similar. Modern philosophers do not generally realize that. They think Plato is speaking only about intellectual beliefs when he disparages opinion. In fact, he is speaking about a state of affairs, a state of consciousness in man, in which all thought and perception is at the mercy of egoistic emotions. Very like Buddhism.

As I launched into my answer to Eric and as I excitedly began making new connections between ideas, I caught a glimpse of his eyes. I was stunned. My God, there was a person there in those eyes. And I was not speaking to that person, or to any person.

I was suspended between seeing the person and being drawn into ideas. It was a moment of great intensity, great reality. Somewhere, somehow, I understood this moment and was grateful for it. I saw that I was in fact in between two movements in myself, two major aspects of my own being. In short, I myself was in question. I saw that these two movements had no relationship to each other.

All this took place, as it were, outside of time, in between words, in between thoughts.

But, of course, I had to go on. Feebly, I tried to stay aware of the person, by looking at him while I spoke. As the words went on, however, as the ideas continued to connect with each other, I kept sensing myself disappearing as though into a cloud. Time and again I would come back to myself and try to speak to the person before me. But even when I was able to look directly at Eric, my attention would immediately be absorbed by the cloud of thoughts.

Although I was disturbed by this, the shock of realizing that I was not speaking *to* anyone was far outweighed by the intense interest I felt in the meaning of these movements. The question of man's two natures, of my own two natures, had actually appeared here in the midst of a living, moving situation. As always, it was a stunningly new discovery.

And now here was Wendy Behrens standing by my desk waiting for me after the class was over. In her hand she was clutching one of the books I had placed on reserve: the *Bhagavad Gita*. I remembered my resolve to get to know these students individually, and set aside my thoughts about the event that had just taken place. Yet my meeting with Wendy was soon to bring the significance of this event into sharp focus.

Wendy is the only student in the class whom one might call troublesome. She often comes in late and is usually the chief culprit in launching the class into occasional spasms of giggling and chattering. Her posture is almost always a profound and defiant slouch, legs sprawled out in front of her, spine at forty-five degrees, head aslant or slung backward, eyes rolling around, looking at the ceiling while the wisecracks and running commentary pour from her as from a horn of plenty. Her brain works at a higher rpm than that of anyone in the class, with the possible exception of Eric Koppleman's.

I like her very much. Apart from simply involuntarily liking her, I find she is a useful barometer—up to a point. When Wendy is quiet, it is a sure sign something real is happening in the class. But, as I say, only up to a point. Sometimes she is simply an obstruction.

Because of Wendy, I have already discovered something important to me about the whole enterprise of speaking seriously to young people, something I had not seen so clearly in my years of teaching at the college level.

When a student in the class is restless or complaining or chattering to a neighbor, my habit has been to interrupt my train of thought and try to bring the inattentive student back to the subject at hand. Just the other day, after having done that for the fifth or sixth time during the class period, I tried something else. Why, I asked myself, should my own attention always be so drawn away by whichever member of the class happened, at a given moment, to be behaving the most outrageously? I don't remember what I was speaking about—it may have been the Buddhist idea of non-attachment—but at a crucial moment in my presentation Wendy started making faces at the particular student in whose direction I was looking. That particular girl, a lively redhead named Heidi, averted her eyes from me, looked at Wendy, and returned to me with an embarrassed grin spread all over her face, which was now as red as her hair. I went on speaking in Heidi's direction, but as always happens in such cases, all force drained out of what I was saying. For the first time, however, I was neatly struck by the absurdity of speaking about something serious into a silly adolescent face. Instead of trying to get the student interested, I simply passed my eyes to the student next to her, which happened to be Sim.

This time even Sim, my "pet," was not paying particularly good attention. His own eyes were darting back and forth between Wendy and Heidi, and I could see he was working hard at suppressing a smile. And so I swiveled to the next student, and to the next, quickly and evenly surveying the whole class until I found a face with attention in it. It was this face I spoke to, while retaining some awareness of the restlessness of some of the other students. When, inevitably, the face I was speaking to began to lose its openness, I quietly moved on again, and again, always directing myself to the face with the most feeling in it.

The results were excellent. Not only did my ideas develop in a normal sequence, but the emotions of the rambunctious students died down all by themselves quickly and naturally. And the general level of the attention in the class remained rich in texture. The same thing happened right at the end of the class, again with Wendy, who, instead of making clownish faces this time, was overcome by a sulking, impatient self-pity about something or other. Again, I resisted the impulse to get her out of it by concentrating on Sim, who by now had regained his usual expression of wonderment.

I promised myself to explore this whole approach fully in the future, both for what it could teach me about young people's wish for serious ideas and the automatic forms of resistance to that wish, but also for what it could teach me in general about the emotions in myself and the unnecessary amount of attention one gives them.

However, the question that emerged from today's class, the question of speaking to the person behind the face, seems for the moment of overriding importance.

And so here is Wendy standing by my desk. Today she is not dressed in old jeans. Is it because of our appointment? She is wearing a dark blue dress, crisp and feminine, and lipstick, unusual for her. Today she is a woman.

"I am going to get to know her," I said to myself. But where to go? I do not have an office here and, in any case, I don't want the environment of the school to intrude.

There is a nice little park about two blocks from the school; I'll take her there and we'll sit on a bench and talk.

It was a typical October day in San Francisco: hot sun, clear air, everything green as summer.

"I see you've chosen one of the books," I said.

She takes her copy of the *Bhagavad Gita* from her book bag and handles it as though it were a block of wood. She thumbs the pages unconvincingly. I decide not to ask her why she has chosen that particular book because she has obviously not chosen it at all. She mumbles something about her interest in studying foreign cultures and says that in one of her classes last semester she did a report on an African dance troupe. She then purses her lips prettily and stops talking, waiting for me to go on with the interview.

I haven't the faintest idea how to go on. What have I gotten myself into? Somehow or other, I start the conversation again and soon find myself listening to descriptions of Wendy's older brother who is now a first-year law student. I also hear about her family's plans to drive to Baja California over the Christmas holidays. Then I hear her own plans to visit several East Coast colleges to which she is thinking of applying.

I ask her what she considers the most important thing in her life and immediately feel like biting my tongue. I see the lies start to form in the expression of her face. Of course they do; *she has no "most important thing" in her life*—why should she? But it's too late. She fabricates something about wanting to be free from oppression and yet self-controlled, or something like that. I have made her lie, or reinforced a lie in her.

Now she goes on, unreeling her "experiences," each more trivial—that is, adolescent—than the one before. Is it fair to say that? She confesses her heart's desire of wanting to travel through Europe "on her own," "feeling the pulse of other cultures."

She is watching me as closely as I am watching her and she is made uncomfortable by my unspoken reactions. I cannot help myself; I then pretend to be more interested in her experiences than I am. Inside, I am amazed by two things: the emptiness and artificiality of Wendy's personal world and my own prior ignorance of this fact. And yet I like her enormously, even more now than before. I look into her eyes and there is a person there. What is a person? Something raw, unformed, and tremendous; something intensely living and intelligent lies behind that smooth, rounded face. It has nothing whatever to do with her "experiences."

In that moment I understand something about education. Or, rather, I let go of something I have long believed in. I have always liked to think that, ideally, education means to bring something out that is already in the person, as opposed to stuffing something into the person, such as information, automatic manners, etc. What was to be led out (*e ducere*) was knowledge or understanding that is contained as a seed in every human being. (Historically, the derivation of the term is not so positive. In the Middle Ages, education was the drawing out of "devils," false beliefs.)

Whether good things or bad things, education had to do with what is in the student to begin with. This view I have shared with many people, professional educators and others, who draw a sharp distinction between teaching necessary skills and information and this other more profound meaning of education.

After speaking to Wendy, I can no longer accept this distinction so simply. A teenager, she still wears her artificiality and lies like she wears her blue dress and lipstick—awkwardly, uncomfortably, transparently. I see her in a year or even six months from now—no longer wobbling on her high heels, the lies she has been encouraged to tell about herself now carefully trimmed and fashioned to last a lifetime. She will become "interesting," that is, a good liar. She will begin to "find her identity," that formation which captures all her own psychic energy and which draws all the attention of those who meet her. Now, I can still see the light of a person behind her face and I know she vaguely senses this light in herself as well. This division of attention in her and in my perception of her makes us both uncomfortable. This discomfort is the last, natural call in man of the Question "Who am I?" just before it becomes completely covered over by the Problem of "establishing one's identity."

I do not know very much about childhood. But I know now one undoubted fact about adolescence. It is a time when the Question of myself is a natural companion, a light that soon flickers and goes out. Often, it is simply degraded under the term "self-consciousness," in its negative sense. No wonder the legends of adolescence are so strange to us: the power to see the mythic unicorn that vanishes when innocence is lost. The unicorn is the person, the single one, the holy individual. To see the unicorn is to experience the Question by sensing the person in myself alongside the social self in all its powerful unreality.

No, I cannot accept that the education of young people involves bringing out what is already in them. On the contrary, something has to be put in! But what? And how? What is the food of that young light, that unformed light within them? How to speak to the personality so that the person also hears?

"Why the *Bhagavad Gita?*" I ask Wendy, groping in the dark. Before she can answer, however, I go on. "I wonder if that's the right book for you." I am acting a part. What else can I do for her? I refuse to tell her that hundreds of millions of people for thousands of years have guided their lives by the ideas in that book. That would only induce in her reactions of pseudorespect, or fear of not understanding, or some kind of defiance. Yet I do wish "to put into her" an attitude toward ideas that will help her feel the scale of the *Bhagavad Gita*. I don't care whether or not I do justice to the book (it can protect itself); I only want to do justice to the person behind the personality of Wendy Behrens.

And so I continue to "act" in order to communicate my own attitude toward the book. I look directly at her, pretending to size up her suitability for the book. She knows she is being weighed, but she doesn't know with respect to what. "I took a big risk putting that book on the shelf," I say. "I knew that whoever chose it would start asking me all sorts of questions that I can't answer. Then they would get angry at me, or disappointed in me."

"What kind of questions?" says Wendy.

"Well, for example, whoever reads that book is certain to start badgering me about why God, or Krishna, as he is called, tells the man in search of wisdom, Arjuna, that he must go out and fight and kill, and then turns around and tells him that he has no power to do anything because the events of life are all foreordained! Is there free will or isn't there?

"Or they will certainly pester me with unanswerable questions about the Infinite, how the whole universe of stars and galaxies and every living thing is merely a speck of dust in the Mind of the Absolute.

"And then there is all that about desires and pleasures and pain—why Krishna dismisses all that as unreal when experience teaches us that the things we can see and touch are real. Is our life only a dream? If so, should we wake up or just go on dreaming?

"And death—what about that? Have we lived before? Will we be reborn after we die? Or is this life and this body all there is? Or do we have a soul and is it immortal? Why do we have to die? Why do we live at all?"

I stopped. The sun passed behind a small cloud and there was a sudden chill in the air. Wendy is now sitting quite still. She is no longer a woman. Nor merely a child. All artifice has fallen away from her face. We both turn our eyes toward the vista of the city spread out before us. The questions I expressed have touched me with unexpected poignancy. I am no longer "a professor." And there is no sense of separation between me and Wendy. When the sun reappears we both quietly get up and, with a few polite words, go our separate ways.

What is this power of questioning that brings people together in such an extraordinary way?

October 22

Today it was Sim. I had been looking forward to this meeting for weeks. Something about Sim has attracted and intrigued me from the beginning. At first, I thought it was only his appearance—the Kirghiz eyes with their suggestion of Asiatic calm set in a very American face. But it was more than that. Sim has plunged into every idea headfirst without protecting himself. His openness, his vulnerability to serious questions set him apart even from the brilliant Eric Koppleman. With new ideas, Sim is like a mariner who wants to inhabit every new land that comes into view. Eric carefully weighs anchor, diligently explores new terrain, and then returns to ship by nightfall.

But today there is something troubling Sim and he is strangely reticent. Walking with him toward the park, I learn that there has been a death in the family—his grandmother. The funeral had been on the weekend; this is his first day back at school and it has been difficult for him.

The park is unusually crowded today. The playground area near the benches is filled with little children shouting and squealing. Sim and I find a place as far away from the bustle as possible, but even so we are frequently interrupted by tiny tots or large, friendly dogs.

What is troubling Sim is not so much the death of his grandmother, as the grieving of his father. His grandmother was apparently quite old, well into her nineties. She died suddenly, without any long illness or gradual decline, and so it was a great shock for the whole family on the morning, six days before, that she failed to come down for breakfast. When Sim saw her in death, his first reaction was that it was not his grandmother lying there. As he tells it, the person in the bed was like a statue, a piece of stone. His grandmother, he felt, had simply gone away. He could not believe anything had died.

His father, usually so strong and capable, was apparently inconsolable. Sim had never seen anyone cry like that, and so often. Seated in the living room or around the dining table, his father would all of a sudden put his head down and his whole body would begin to shake convulsively. This could happen anywhere, any time. To Sim, this manifestation was more inexplicable than death itself.

In the midst of this account, which evoked such sharp memories of my own first encounters with death, Sim asked, in a voice almost entirely free of emotion, "At the cemetery, when the coffin was being covered with soil, my father recited a prayer praising God. And I had to recite it, too. Why is that? I didn't feel like praising God for creating death. And my father was crying when he praised God. If you ask me, I think he must have been hating God at that moment."

Sim turned his head and looked directly at me. "Dr. Needleman," he said, "why does death make people weak?"

I could hardly believe my ears. I thought I knew all the kinds of questions people ask about death.

I turned away from Sim's wide-open face. Were there really any ideas or thoughts about death that were as deep as that question? Was I supposed to pretend that I was any stronger than Sim's father or anyone else? I found myself saying, "Real feeling is not weakness, Sim."

The moment I said that, I understood something about the need for philosophy in the life of everyone, young or old. There are ideas that increase or deepen feeling, and there are ideas that draw us away from feeling. The subject of death must always be part of real philosophy—but in order to deepen the feeling, not in order to remove it.

"You know," I continued, "the ancient philosophers taught that the world we live in is impermanent and constantly changing. Always and everywhere there is birth and death, coming-into-being and passing-out-of-being. We've been talking about this in our discussions of Plato, do you remember?"

Sim nodded.

"But Plato also spoke of something else," I said, "that doesn't change."

"You mean the eternal ideas," said Sim. "The Good, Justice, Beauty . . ."

I interrupted him. "Think of them as laws of the universe. Everything changes, but the laws never change. Everything obeys fundamental laws. Everything."

"Isn't that what science says, too?"

"Yes, but science has only discovered the laws of material objects. They haven't yet discovered the laws that govern life and death, nor the laws of the mind."

"Then," said Sim, "that means that death is not the strongest thing in the universe."

I waited for Sim to complete his thought.

"The laws are stronger. Even death has to obey the laws?"

The conversation that followed lasted a long time. I remember being surprised when we got up to leave that the sun was already touching the horizon.

It was the connection between death and law that touched Sim so strongly. Death is omnipresent and inevitable; Sim, like everyone, understood that fact. Because he understood that fact, he was able to represent to himself that a law of the universe is also omnipresent and inevitable and—this was new for him—a law of the universe is real and substantial, more so than the objects and things and beings one sees and deals with every moment of the day.

Sim and I discussed the tragedy of human thought, which contains the cultural residue of formulations and symbols representing the idea of the goodness of all existence, but which at the same time is cut off from directly perceiving the laws of the universe. The goodness of the laws, as the ancient philosophers taught, is seen only in the laws of mind and life. These laws can themselves only be known through observing how life actually works and how the energies of the mind actually work. These are the laws of creation and transformation, which Pythagoras represented through the science of music and mathematical symbol.

How far we were from the desiccated problem of universals, as the scholastic philosophers of the Middle Ages termed this issue and as it has survived, in an increasingly embalmed state, in the contemporary era. And how strange that so many of us can understand that all things obey laws and yet believe that material things are the basic reality.

Idealists believe in a nonmaterial reality, but do not experience the laws as they actually work. Materialists believe in things perceived or inferred on the basis of the external senses, but cannot account for the laws that material things obey, not to mention the laws that the mind and everything living obeys.

It was Sim who made the connection between the idea of law and God. "Is praising God the same thing as praising the laws of the universe?" he asked.

I replied by recalling for both of us what Plato said to a society in which the whole idea of God had been engulfed by superstition. Man cannot see the goodness of the laws if his mind is drugged by the love of pleasure and the fear of pain. Such a mind, Plato taught, invents gods or denies them, but never sees the laws at all. I said that, as I understand the ancient philosophy, "to know God is to know the laws. And to feel the goodness of the laws is to praise God." But I added: "It is difficult for man to feel the goodness of the laws when he is suffering." I wanted to go on. I wanted to say how the whole question was beginning to appear to me in that moment. I began to understand that the essence of this whole question was contained in a saying that I once heard somewhere, I don't remember by whom: "When you think something, remember God; when you feel something, remember His laws."

The idea of God is for the intellect so that, when the intellect is active, a man will not forget to feel his need and his individual place in the scheme of things; the idea of cosmic law is for the emotions so that, when the emotions are active, a man will not forget that knowledge is necessary. Thus, in the Hebrew prayer for the dead the mourner is first reminded of the universal laws of creation and destruction.

While I was discussing these difficult matters with Sim, I saw that he was actually following only a little of the line of inquiry. Yet his face was burning with interest and attention. His face was radiant. In that face, I saw my own inner state. These questions were above me, too. But is that not what we wish, what we need? We were both being stretched, intellectually and emotionally, by a real question and by the shadow of a real idea.

"I can understand," said Sim, "that death is necessary. Things have to die to make room for other things to be born. But why did it have to be that way? And . . . just because it's necessary, does it make it good? And . . . even if it is necessary and also good, how can the thing that is dying believe it is good? Nobody wants to die, do they? Animals never want to die. People never want to die, do they? I don't want to die, even if it is necessary."

I could not take my eyes from Sim's face. Where was the problem that had troubled me so in class and then with Wendy, the problem of the person and the thought, the division between them? The problem had disappeared. Was I speaking to a question in the form of a person, or to a person in the form of a question? Sim did not have this question; he *was* this question.

And so was I. I, too, fear death and I felt it then, speaking to Sim. I will not pretend that I can stand above this fear and call forth some grand idea that will dissolve it. We are both afraid and at the same time we wish to understand. In that state, we—either of us—could perhaps hear the Socrates of the *Apology* telling the Athenian state that he will not choose to live without pursuing the search for understanding. Would I rather live and never understand, or die and understand?

I think I know what is happening here. The fear of death is not being covered over by some majestic philosophy of immortality, nor is this fear being buffered by logical puzzles about defining death and the self; nor is it being assuaged by warming death up with poetics and therapeutics, nor is it being accepted with either resignation or defiance in some Emersonian haze, existentialist nightmare, or humanistic daydream. The fear of death is being met by the wish to understand; and perhaps that wish is the only thing in human life that is as strong as death, or that can become as strong as death. It is *eros*. No wonder Plato called it the bridge between man and immortality.

I think of the story of Al-Hallaj, the great Sufi saint of tenth-century Persia. He was sentenced to die for heresy: his skin was slowly stripped away from his body and, scourged and mutilated, he was hung upon a cross to await his death. That much is historical fact. Al-Hallaj had sung of his identity with God—a heretical notion to the Muslim orthodoxy. Some say that he openly sought martyrdom by speaking in this way. Make of that what one will, a story of his last days was once told to me when I myself was in a condition of great distress.

It was told to me in the most pedestrian of places—a crowded businessman's cafeteria in New York—on a freezing winter day when it seemed that the sun would never again appear from behind iron-gray clouds.

"When Al-Hallaj was on the cross, his pupils came to him to hear his last words of instruction."

I asked myself, what would be the last words of a martyred saint: an exhortation to faith? a vision of God? a command of forgiveness?

"As he was dying, he said one thing to them."

One thing? What? A blessing of some sort? Peace? Love? Nothing of the kind. Amid the clattering of plates and the confusing buzz of laughing and loud voices, the words struck me as though in my chest: "Study yourself."

I came out of these thoughts to see Sim enjoying a completely transformed mood. Throughout our conversation dogs of every shape and size were constantly passing by or cavorting in front of us or nudging our feet. A big, lumpy spaniel of some sort had finally drawn Sim's attention by trotting up to us carrying a stick in his mouth, which he soberly dropped in Sim's lap as though fulfilling a sacred mission. Sim was now teasing him playfully with the stick and finally could resist no longer, but stood up and heaved the stick far into the distance. The spaniel charged after it, as did about ten other dogs who were lurking nearby. Sim watched the raucous race for the stick with the same rapt attention with which he had asked about life and death. In no time, our bench was surrounded by more dogs than I have ever seen in one place in my life, each generously contributing its decibels to the production of total cacophony. The moment Sim picked up the retrieved stick and prepared to throw it again, the barking stopped instantly as the dogs tensely waited and watched. Noticing this, Sim lowered it and just as suddenly the racket started up again. Sim was completely delighted with this discovery. At the precise instant he raised the stick above the level of his knees the barking stopped cold and the dogs became as silent as monks. Sim played like this for quite a while and I laughingly put my thoughts away. *Eros* may be a force that is stronger than death but, in us poor mortals who philosophize on park benches, it cannot withstand even one friendly dog.

After Sim got bored playing with the dogs, we turned to the so-called real reason for our meeting—selection of the text that Sim should work on for the semester report. I had no doubt what it should be: Plato's *Apology*. I told Sim so, without hesitation. I couldn't tell him the story of Al-Hallaj; it would mean little to him at this point in his life. But if he is anything like I was at his age, and I think he is, he will be enthralled by a properly guided reading of the trial of Socrates. It is there that the divine commandment to "know thyself" is introduced into the current of Western culture as something that is equal to and even stronger than the fact of death.

Ah, but who reads the *Apology* in this way anymore? In my own life and thought, the luminous paradox of Socrates' death flickered and was nearly extinguished countless times by academic explanations. The same thing is true for many people. For many of us, it has remained, as it were, just beneath the level of consciousness like the great myths of old were intended to do, slowly giving off its radiation over the years until, at a certain stage of life, the richness of its meaning begins to erupt within us and support the search for imperishable truth.

I know how Sim's study of the *Apology* will proceed, if he is anything like I was. In the first place, he has already heard the standard "gossip" about Socrates—that here was a wise man who was sentenced to death by the establishment and refused to compromise merely in order to save his life. He will have heard that Socrates believed it was more important to obey the laws of the state than to save one's own life. Therefore, even as he begins to read the *Apology* carefully, he will have the paradox already in his mind: Why would a wise man choose to die for the sake of such a relative thing as civic order?

In a way, it is more puzzling even than the death of Jesus, who, according to the "gossip," was God or the Son of God and, as it were, could "bank" on his own resurrection. But Socrates does not claim to be God or the Son of God. He speaks of the gods, but he says only that he doesn't even know if there is life after death. He is not sure; no one can be sure. And yet . . . and yet: Something takes the place of God for Socrates. But it is not called God. Something produces in Socrates a certainty about life and death, but it is not called exactly "faith in immortality," and it seems to exist in him even alongside his professed uncertainty. His uncertainty about immortality seems paradoxically of one piece with his certainty. How can that be? And what really takes the place of "God" for him?

If Sim is like me, he will on his own start reading the other dialogues dealing with the death of Socrates. And the paradox will only grow deeper. He will study the *Phaedo*, which reports the last hours of Socrates' life—a discussion dealing with the very subject of immortality. And he will see the proofs of immortality offered by Socrates refuted on logical grounds by the pupils, and will not be convinced even by the last proof, which the pupils accept. Here the soul is defined as a principle of harmony, that which harmoniously orders all the functions within the human structure. Logically, nothing is proved. Yet the harmony of Socrates himself, the unbreakable presence of Socrates, shines through the logical charade. What produces this presence in Socrates? What is the nature of his being? It is *inquiry* itself, out of which arises not only the freedom to use and then let go of logic, but a certain precise compassion for others and the power to look directly at one's own death.

Sim will discover, or feel, that the God of Socrates is self-knowledge, self-inquiry. It is at this point that guidance is needed. If I can succeed in communicating to him even a small fraction of the richness of content in the Socratic commandment to "know thyself," I will consider that I have done something of service for him. I wish to spare him the years in which that phrase was exiled into a corner of my own mind far away from real connection with the rest of my life and aspirations.

The Athenian court would have gladly exiled Socrates to a

far country, but he would not accept that. Are we not like the Athenian court ourselves? To us, the phrase "self-knowledge" means little more than "psychologizing" about ourselves; that is, obtaining emotionally stimulating opinions about ourselves, against the background of the view of human nature insinuated into us by our own abnormal social order.

Or it means conceptual analysis, which cannot penetrate into our emotions and body because the faculty of thinking itself is encapsulated within us. Thoughts about myself have no penetrating action upon the emotions and instincts.

Socratic self-knowledge is self-attention, which is a force that can exist and act with tremendous power within ourselves. For Socrates, it develops and grows in relationship to the various functions of the whole human structure, in the midst of the "citizens of Athens," in "the marketplace."

Socrates is a presence, an attention that can look directly at death.

In that direction, so I have come to understand, lies the solution of the paradox of the death of Socrates. How else to understand that everything Socrates died for is brought together under the heading of the commandment to "know thyself." The laws that govern this great range of energy within the self are the laws that govern everything that exists within the universe. These are the laws that come from God, and are symbolized in the *Apology* as the Laws of the State. Plato speaks of them as the Ideas. They are all within myself, only I must search for them, and this search itself must obey these laws. The Ideas are the laws of God, the laws of Mind, the laws of Being.

As we were about to get up and leave, Sim came back to the matter of his father's grief. "Is there anything I can do to help him?" Sim asked.

While I was weighing that question in my mind, I thought

that I would like very much to meet this interesting young man's parents and see what they were like.

"Yes," I said, "I think there is something you can do. In the first place, don't automatically think of what your father is going through as a weakness. In other times and in other cultures the period of mourning was often considered very sacred and people would come to the mourner to receive his blessing, or to ask for his help for themselves. The anxiety about death is not at all the same thing as the confrontation with death. They are two completely different kinds of suffering. The second kind of suffering is a painful confrontation between what people imagine about life and the real laws of life itself, which, as we've said, is another word for God. This kind of suffering brings wisdom and compassion."

"What about the other kind of suffering?" Sim asked.

"Well," I said, "what is the opposite of wisdom?"

Sim thought for a moment. "But how can that be?" he said. "People die all the time, all over the world. So, how come so few people have wisdom?"

"Try to find out what Plato says about that," I answered. "That kind of suffering doesn't automatically bring wisdom. People have to want wisdom beforehand, otherwise, it just turns into the first kind of suffering, which brings the opposite of wisdom. They have to want it very much. They have to learn how to look for it, how to inquire after it—that's what Socrates taught.

"What's the name of this desire?" I asked Sim, after a pause.

"What do you mean?"

"Sim, where have you been? What's the name that Plato gives to this desire, this love of wisdom?"

Sim's face brightened. "Philosophy!" he said. But then his narrow Kirghiz eyes narrowed further. "But my father isn't a philosopher!"

I laughed. "Don't be so sure," I said. "A philosopher isn't just someone who reads books and takes courses."

That ended our conversation. Walking back to the school, Sim cheerfully talks nonstop and I realize that my work with these young people is not going to be complete until I get to know their parents as well.

November 12

In the past three weeks I have managed to meet at least once with every student in the class. I now see very clearly that it is not a matter of distinguishing which of them are open to the questions of philosophy and which of them are not. No, the task is to see in which *way* they are open. Because the fact of the matter is that they are all, each of them, sensitive to great ideas whether they know it or not.

In one of the classes, discussing the teachings of Hinduism, I told a story that most beautifully illustrates the Hindu doctrine of the great Self within each human being. Only now, knowing these young people, I understand this powerful story in quite a new way.

A female tiger, late in her pregnancy, spies a herd of goats and, charging after them in her awkward condition, she stumbles against a jagged rock. She strikes her head and is killed, but the cub is born.

With the danger passed, the goats return and, seeing the tiny cub, they raise him as their own. The cub begins to grow up, contentedly, as though he were a goat. He feeds on grass and even automatically imitates the bleating sound that goats make. He is quite happy.

All is well until one day another tiger, a great and fierce male tiger, spies the herd. He, too, charges after the herd and the goats flee in panic. The cub, however, does not move. He sees this enormous, awesome being bearing down upon them and he sees all his brothers and sisters running past him, their eyes wild with terror. For some reason that the cub does not understand, he feels no fear whatever, not even when the great tiger passes right next to him.

Seeing the cub there amidst the goats, the tiger is startled and stops in his tracks. "What are *you* doing *here!*" he angrily roars. The cub blinks his eyes and gives out a pathetic, gravelly bleating sound. The tiger cannot believe what he sees and hears, and he roars again in utter disgust. Forgetting about his hunt, he snatches the cub by the scruff of his neck and carries him off into the jungle in his huge jaws. There, by the side of a reflecting pool, he dangles the cub over the water so that he can see his own reflection. "Look at yourself!" growls the tiger. "You see! You are one of *our* tribe!" In fact the cub is astonished to see that he has the same kind of face as this awesome creature who is holding him. But all he can do is give out another bleating, goatlike cry.

Infuriated beyond measure, the great tiger carries the cub to its lair where, in the corner of the cave, there lies an antelope, a fresh kill. The tiger sets the cub down next to the bloody meat and orders him: "Eat!" But the cub, who has never eaten anything but grasses and leaves, the fare of goats, is repelled and refuses with yet another bleating sound. The tiger insists, but the cub is nauseated by the very sight and smell of the raw meat in front of him. Finally, his patience exhausted, the great tiger snatches up the cub in one gigantic paw and forces the meat down the cub's throat. The poor little cub gags and chokes as he involuntarily swallows the new food. Then, suddenly, something remarkable happens. The cub begins to feel a strange and wondrous warmth surging through him, a sensation like nothing he has ever known before. Suffused with this warmth, he cries out in joy and the sound that comes from him is the same roar of the tiger, the sound which every other beast of the jungle trembles to hear.

The great tiger smiles in satisfaction. "Now," he says to the cub, "you know what you are! Come, let us go together to the hunt!"

Better than any dozen lectures or treatises, this story illustrates the idea that within every human being there is God, the great Self, *Atman*, which is *Brahman*: the great *I Am* of man and the universe. But a screen of culturally conditioned fears, desires, and patterns of behavior forms itself around this great Self in every human being. This screen is the ego, the imaginary I, the social identity. The tragedy of human life, the only real tragedy of human life, is that we live and move entirely under the illusion of the ego.

Now I see something new in this story, which speaks of a young tiger, a cub, with all its growth ahead of it. The divinity in man is as yet unformed; it needs to grow. I see that this divinity, this young tiger-nature in us, appears in the form of a seeking, a questioning, a hunger for being and truth. The roar of these high-school children is just that. And it sounds, this roar, in the very midst of every other impulse and manifestation of everyday life; in the midst of the family, work, play, suffering and pleasure, sexual attraction and confusion; in the midst of hatred and love, in building and destroying, in war, in ambition, in grief. Why am I here? What is the meaning of my life on earth? What is the family, what is work, what is science, what is art and religion, why do men kill each other? Why do we die, what is our brain for, how are we different from the animals, what is right and wrong, how can i know, why is there pain and disease—all these questions written in the margins of our lives are really so many expressions of one force, one central movement within the very structure of the human psyche—*eros*, the wish for Being, the striving to become the God known in the ancient traditions as *I Am*.

How readily the class responded to this story! How quick they were to follow it wherever it would lead them! I had only to mention the distinction between goat-values and tiger-values in order to trigger a rapid sequence of comments, questions, argument, and discussion, which, in its way, not only brought together everything we had been discussing until now, but which—to be sure, in ragged and awkward fashion—mirrored the fundamental ideas of all the great philosophies of the ancient world.

Eric Koppleman was first out of the starting gate. "Are there goat-psychiatrists?" he said, with a good-natured laugh. "Suppose the tiger cub was feeling sort of depressed because he couldn't bleat as well as everyone else. Probably he'd be sent to a therapist so that he could learn to adjust."

"But it wouldn't only be the sounds he made," said Lois Kesley. "He wouldn't feel right about anything, really, would he? And he would think it was because he was inferior, when actually the real reason would be that he was superior."

At that, Wendy Behrens stepped in. "But that's not the main point of the story! The point of the story is that he is trained to be a very good goat. He does goat things really well, just like all the other goats around him. Society makes good goats out of tigers!"

"What about his stripes?" said Jeanette Streiser, a slight, dark-haired girl with whom I had met privately just the day before.

"No problem," quipped Eric. "He'd start a fashion in stripes. His friends would start painting stripes on themselves."

Again, Wendy broke in. "No," she said. "They wouldn't even *see* the stripes! They wouldn't see anything of his tiger-nature. Goats only see goats, don't you understand?"

This did not satisfy Jeanette. She had been reading *Her-Bak*, that extraordinary novel of a young initiate among the wise men of ancient Egypt. In our meeting the day before she had told me how struck she was by the kind of dissatisfaction with life felt by the hero of that novel. It put a new light on her own confusions about life. Maybe not all her problems were signs that something was wrong with her. Maybe, she wondered, they were signs that something was right with her.

Whenever Jeanette spoke, she always commanded attention because of her voice, which was startlingly deep and mature in contrast to her frail, birdlike physical appearance. Listening to her, I was struck anew by how young people seem to grow: Suddenly, without warning, one aspect or function breaks into maturity while everything else still remains on the side of childhood. Poor Jeanette, because her voice had developed first, was now identified with that function. Her parents had urged singing and drama lessons upon her and there had even been a little write-up in the Sunday papers about the usually male roles she was taking in a local choral group. In our meeting yesterday I saw that something in her resisted being identified like this as a sort of voice that happened to have a person attached to it. It was not conscious in her, this resistance to forming her identity around her voice. But I saw how many of her problems in life were created by this situation.

Jeanette was known as an unusually multi-faceted student. She was on two varsity athletic teams, she was always involved in charity drives, she worked on the school paper, as well as being a successful student academically. This, too, was encouraged by her parents, who wanted her to be well-rounded. Yet she told me— and I could see it very clearly without her having to tell me at all—that when she started thinking about life under the influence of a large philosophical question, a tremendous tension seemed, for a moment, to give way. "Philosophy makes me feel like I'm coming home," she said to me.

Perhaps it was my meeting with her that had helped me to understand a new meaning of this story from the Hindu tradition. The divinity which man is born with is a movement toward internal balance of all the functions within the human structure. This movement takes place under the form of self-questioning, guided by ideas that refer to a tremendous scale of reality. This movement is the tiger cub; the far goal, the immensity of a completely balanced human nature, is the tiger himself, the great Self.

Such questioning is a suffering of a special kind, quite unlike the suffering that attends the effort to fit our lives into our "goat" identity. Although such questioning is certainly suffering, it is accompanied by a distinct intimation of release and homecoming. I do not know who I am, but I am not what my society tells me I am. The experience and act of this questioning is itself the tiger-nature as it begins its growth.

What intrigued Jeanette about the story was that the cub is always just that, a tiger cub. He really has no intrinsic qualities of the goat. He is a tiger, but he does not know it. How can that be?

It intrigues me, too. I see the power of great ideas to start and support this special sort of questioning in young people. I see how easily and naturally it comes to them. Yet, without the help of such ideas presented to them in a definite way, this questioning may never get started or never move them very far. Yet, at least before they are "fully grown adults" with a "secure identity role" in society, this questioning is there all the time, like the tiger-nature, like the stripes of the cub. But who sees it? Who honors this questioning? Who supports it in our world?

I have been wondering at the power of ideas, that by them-selves they seem to have a moral effect on people's lives. I see now, too, that it is the self-interrogation evoked by such ideas that produces this moral effect. We have taught our young people ideas in a way that actually blunts this moral power of ideas. This failure needs to be corrected and it can be corrected, of this I am sure. Otherwise, true ideas simply do not and cannot penetrate into us. Socrates understood this.

I began, today, to look at all these students in the way I was seeing Jeanette. Jeanette was a "voice." Something was *forming* around that function in her, an identity that would carry her through marriage, career, motherhood, through pain and illness, through all the achievements and failures, through the pleasures and shocks that are the lot of every human being. However, with-out the help of true ideas—whether in the expressions of real philosophy, or in a kind of art that transmits silence, or in religious symbols that call from another scale of reality—that identity-formation will gradually, but inexorably, tighten into the noose we call "character."

If Jeanette is a "voice," then Eric is a "brain"; Lois, with her wide eyes, is a "sigh"; Wendy, despite all her infectious vitality, is a "complaint." And Sim? Is he not a sort of *charm*? Look at how expertly he makes everyone like him, how some tremendous intelligence and sensitivity is constantly employed to that end, and how blank he becomes when this is not at issue, whether with respect to people, concepts, or physical tasks. I've seen him in his car, an old Volkswagen, and I swear even his car likes him. Like Jeanette's voice, Sim's charm—which comes from I know not what emotional and mental centers in his psyche—has developed in front of everything else in him.

Perhaps I am wrong, perhaps I do not see these young people clearly enough. I cannot help but envision the whole of their lives as so many scripts that are now, just on the brink of adulthood, being cast into their final, revised form before being put into production.

Jeanette could not accept Wendy and Eric's interpretation of the story; she could not accept that the cub would be completely absorbed by the society of the goats and not have the slightest intimation of its own real nature. But it was easy enough for Eric to answer every objection she raised. Either the goat-psychiatrists would "cure" the cub of its "insecurity about itself" or the "goat public" would award it a prize for "unusual abilities" or the "goat-priests" would instill so much guilt in the cub that it would strive to become an even better goat than the goats themselves.

And so the discussion proceeded. If the cub was happy as a goat, why should the tiger interfere? What is happiness? Can you be really happy if you are not what you are meant to be? Besides, when the cub actually tastes the meat, it knows a kind of happiness far greater than anything it has previously experienced. (When that point was made by one of the students, I was tempted to unreel a discussion of Book IX of the *Republic* where Plato speaks of the unique quality of joy that accompanies the taste of real understanding. But I restrained myself.)

When the three o'clock bell rang, the subject of "goat morality" had gripped the class. Eric had shrewdly identified the cub as Nietzsche's "superman," beyond the good and evil of the goat world. No sooner had he done so than the whole attitude of the class toward the story changed. Their unbridled delight in tracing out the consequences of the simile passed into disturbance and discomfort. No matter what he was—goat, tiger, or whatever—it would never be right to kill, to destroy, to cause pain. On the other hand, goat morality could be identified as the "herd morality" of Nietzsche, selfishness masquerading as piety, laziness masquerading as altruism, greed pretending to be individualism, license decked out as freedom and liberty. Finally, the discussion came to a sort of climactic point when Lois and Heidi, almost at the same moment, asked if the cub didn't after all owe something to the goats!

The school day was over. Students from the other classes were running by the door; there was much shouting and motion in the schoolyard. At the sound of the bell several of the students had automatically started gathering up their books to leave. But everyone was still in their places and remained there in the silence that followed Lois's and Heidi's question.

I said nothing. I waited. An entirely new quality had appeared in everyone's face and comportment. There was the spontaneous interest in a serious question about man—and right alongside that there were the impulses to get up and leave—to go to basketball practice, to go out for an ice-cream cone, to meet a friend, to study for an exam. A tremendous tension filled the room, extraordinarily alive and creative and still. I tried to do nothing to indicate in which direction they should move, which side of themselves they should obey. I knew that at any moment this state of inbetweenness would dissolve and the whole class, including myself, would become "goats." But for now, they were indeed young tigers experiencing, without knowing it, the space between their two natures. They were philosophers.

It was Sim through whom the moment ended. Was he reading my mind? He had been uncharacteristically silent throughout the discussion, his face darkening as it proceeded. Now, suddenly, his features relaxed and his eyes filled with light.

"The cub," he said, "is both a tiger and a goat!"

"Go on," I said.

"Even though he was born with the genetic code of a tiger, he has the ability to imitate a goat, right? Therefore . . ."

A wave of relaxation passed over everyone. After a pause, Sim continued: "Therefore, the story doesn't end in the tiger's lair. The cub grows up and instead of hunting down the goats, he returns to them in order to help them. And . . . from that day on, the tigers and the goats live together in harmony!"

The class practically cheered. In a body, they all got up to leave, laughing and joking. As they were leaving, Eric quipped at Sim, "Then what do the tigers eat after that?"

"Vegetables," said Jeanette, racing out of the room.

CHAPTER 7

Parents

Toward the end of November, I spoke to a group of parents interested in learning about my work at the school. When I agreed to meet with them, however, I had made it clear that it would be too soon to draw even tentative conclusions about the role of philosophy in the education of children. Instead, I would speak to them about philosophy in general, why it was needed in modern life. I had no way of knowing that by the end of November not only would I have come to *very* definite conclusions about philosophy and young people, but that I would be ready to make detailed recommendations to anyone willing to listen to me, as well as offer substantial commitments of my own time.

However, I decided to stick to my original plan and avoid describing what was going on in the classroom. I had several reasons for this decision. In the first place, as I have already mentioned, my private meeting with Sim made me want very much to meet the parents of these children in order to see for myself what sort of influences existed in their households. I had come to the rather firm conclusion that in order to "get to know" anyone, anyone at all, it is necessary to see a person's relationship to ideas.

This latter opinion of mine was the source of some dispute with friends in the field of psychiatry and psychology. They spoke of "personality types," using one or another system of psychological classification—from Freud, Jung, Sheldon, or other modern theorists of human behavior. They spoke of projective tests, such as the Rorschach or the Thematic Apperception Test. They spoke of phenomenological analysis in order to ascertain another person's "original project" or "world-design." They spoke of childhood traumas and "significant adults" as being fundamental determining factors in the shaping of personality. While I, to their annoyance, spoke of one thing only: the orientation toward ideas. I did not deny that people were different from one another in the ways that my psychological colleagues said. I only claimed that what they were concerned about was of secondary importance in understanding the differences between people. However, I'm afraid I was not very tactful about my point of view. In effect, what I argued was that the whole of modern psychology had systematically ignored the most important aspect of human nature.

They, in turn, accused me of being superficial. "Aren't you simply speaking about what we would call 'interests' or 'preferences'?" said one. "Some people are interested in philosophy, some are interested in art or music or science or making money. How can you compare that with the attempt to understand the deeper, psychodynamic forces at work in different individuals?"

But, of course, I was not speaking of any such thing. There is art that expresses ideas and art that only satisfies the desire for stimulation; there is music that evokes the longing for truth and there is the music of sentiment, intellectual innovation, or sex; there is science that arises out of wonder and there is science that solves material problems; even the making of money can serve two fundamentally different purposes—the search for understanding or the desire for power, prestige, and possessions. A man's relationship to ideas is not measured only by his interest in the verbal formulation of ideas that is conventionally termed "philosophy." Moreover, ideas need not be known only with the intellectual function; they can be felt and sensed as well. One man loves wisdom with the instrument of his mind, another with his emotions, and another with his body.

Development, I argued, is a matter of loving wisdom with more and more parts of the human machine and has nothing to

do with "oral, anal, and genital"; nor with Jungian "individua-
tion"; nor with "adaptive behavior." Needless to say, I did not
succeed in making my motives understood to many of my colleagues in the field of psychology.

My talk was scheduled for 8 p.m. in the school library and
nothing else that happened that evening surpassed in intensity my
first impression as I entered the library. No doubt the shock I
experienced was in part due simply to the incongruity of all these
adults milling around in a room designed for young people. The
tables and chairs were just a little too small for them; the ceiling
just a shade too low; the whole room (which, objectively speaking,
was spacious) seemed cast for a slightly different species of being.
This impression was all the stronger because I arrived late and, by
the time I entered, the atmosphere was more that of a cocktail
party than a lecture. Styrofoam cups containing coffee or white
wine abounded. Cigarette smoke and the sounds of animated conversation filled the room. Attractive, well-dressed men and women
stood in small clumps laughing and chatting.

I was surprised by my own surprise at this scene. Had I come
to regard the school as some kind of monastery? Whatever the
reason, in a very brief period of time I experienced a number of
clear perceptions that could all be summed up by the image of a
group of people gathered together for some shameful purpose, but
whose only form of social behavior was various habitual forms of
superficially gracious mutual respect. It was not unlike—if I may
put it this way—walking into a very high-class brothel where the
cream of society is passing the time engagingly discussing socially
acceptable topics while their hearts are pounding and their eyes
glistening with the private anticipation of some deliciously sinful
experience awaiting them. Only here, of course, what awaited
them was not some sinful behavior, but only a philosophy lecture.

With a cup of wine and a cigarette in my own hands, and
engaged in pleasant conversation with several of the parents, I

began to experience the same thing in myself. Did I really intend to speak about serious ideas concerning the meaning of life and death? How artificial, how embarrassing the prospect seemed to me!

But, I asked myself, what "person" in me has suddenly taken charge of my mind to whom the prospect of considering serious questions seemed artificial? Is not this person "himself" even more artificial? I became extremely interested in this question, even as I chatted and laughed. And in the space of not more than five or ten minutes there unreeled before me an entire cast of "inner persons" for each of whom the prospect of thinking about real questions seemed either distasteful, uninteresting, or frightening.

Surely, this was the "multitude" that Plato speaks about in the *Republic*! These were the "masses," the "merchants, tradesmen, laborers, farmers, 'artists,' cobblers," and so forth, who do not understand the motives of *eros*, the wish for truth, and who must be convinced to submit to the rule of Mind, the "philosopher king."

Here I am standing and chatting with a strikingly attractive woman in her mid-thirties. Sexual thoughts arise in me as I am speaking about something or other. This "person" who wants to have sex—what does "he" care about self-knowledge or consciousness? Next to this woman stands a white-haired man well-known in the business community. I would like to become a "genuine friend" of this man—and why? Because becoming his "genuine friend" might result in some money for me. This "person" who is always looking for money, he is alarmed at the prospect of trying to speak about truth in an honest way.

A second woman, also attractive, joins our little *tête-à-tête*. I make a witty remark that brings a round of laughter and I—or should I say "he"?—am bathed in a sensation of such all-pervading warmth that I feel almost like a god. This witty, scintillating "person," standing at the center of an admiring group of people: Doesn't he find real philosophy rather heavy and pretentious?

As I took my seat in front of the group in order to begin the lecture, I was forcibly struck by a realization. I had come here to get to know the parents of my young students, the adults who had shaped their minds. But all these "adults" were inside me! If I could know them, I could know myself! And I need to know myself. I need to know why the truth that my mind acknowledges has no power in my life. It is the Socratic question again. It is Pythagoras and his school—the question of how to transmit true ideas to all these "adults" in myself who either do not know or do not care about or cannot hear the convictions of the mind.

Is this not a central meaning of the idea of *desire* that has come down to us through the ages not only from Pythagoras and Plato, but from long before even these ancient philosophers? Desires by themselves are perhaps not the enemy that the traditional teachings speak about, but they become quite another thing when they assume in ourselves the status of "I"; when they feel like "myself." These innumerable "myselves"—are they not the reason man *forgets* truth and being?

Then what a colossal error it has been for man to struggle with what he calls *desires* without recognizing this "myself-ing" as his principal enemy!

Sitting there in front of all these "myselves" or parents, I experienced an extraordinary moment, the sort I have had on other occasions. I have not seen such a moment described in any of the mystical literature of the traditional writings and the only way I can describe it is to say that for a brief stretch of time I was inside a living and breathing metaphor. That is, the outer world and the inner world fused together around a specific idea or question. The sense of ecstasy or joy was, perhaps, not less than is reported by some mystics, yet it was not caused by a direct experience of a higher reality, but, on the contrary, by a direct experience of a lower reality, by the unmistakable experience of a question about myself. To put it another way, I experienced the reality of an idea in such a way that a practical, living direction of inquiry opened before me in which my outer activity could be pursued—with no "forcing"—as a mirror or concrete metaphor of my inner search.

Such experiences have provided me with an exact standard by which to ponder the issue of whether or not life has a meaning. Life has a meaning when a new question appears, and when the external circumstances of life arrange themselves as material for the investigation of that question. I am certain that the large, theoretical problem of the purpose of human life on earth can only be approached after one has experienced what it is to have a moment of direction simultaneously in one's inner and outer life.

I have rarely been so clear about any undertaking in my life. 1. I want to understand the nature of the love of truth in man—why it does not penetrate into the life we live, and how it can be made to penetrate; 2. this love and the crystallizing of the obstacles to it can be seen clearly in late adolescence; 3. to understand young people, it is also necessary to know the influences that have acted upon them, especially the influence of their parents; 4. what one most needs to know about these parents is their own relationship to truth—in this case, truth in the form of great ideas; 5. these parents are also in myself.

My lecture to the parents produced one dramatic result which I had hoped for, but did not really expect or intend. Midway through the discussion, several of the parents spontaneously asked me to offer *them* a course in philosophy! I instantly agreed to it.

But how to arrange it? It would be of no interest to conduct a series of intellectual entertainments. All these parents led very full lives—in business, the arts, science, education, charitable and political activities. It would be of no interest for our meetings to be just another cultural activity to round out their already full schedules, adding an evening of philosophy to symphony, theater, etc. If I wanted to study their relationship to ideas I had to arrange conditions correspondingly. My aim was to study, not to teach; or, rather, by teaching philosophy, to study the current status of the attraction to truth in the psyche of highly cultured men and women.

The first step was the sending out of the required announcement, informing all the parents about the course. A mere detail, perhaps, but isn't life made up of such details? Could not my study begin right there? The whole question of human behavior, of living according to what one believes in, can be situated there in man's relationship to details. Philosophy professors can argue all they like about moral action, about how the good can be realized in concrete situations; theologians can prophetically declaim about man's inability to carry out his higher aims; psychologists can offer explanations about why people's acts go against their own best interests. But the whole issue is really contained in the imbalanced attention man gives to ideas, ideals, and aims on the one hand, and the details of living on the other hand.

I settled on the following simple statement:

Several parents have asked me to lead a discussion group in philosophy and I would be very glad to experiment with studying Plato's *Republic* with anyone who is interested. As for my approach to this material, I can say only that I take the study of philosophy as a way of opening up the most elusive and fundamental questions of living: Who are we? And why are we here?

I was glad to see this little statement jammed in the middle of a page filled with other announcements and news items being sent out to all the parents. If there was even the tiniest element of a *call to the search* in my statement, I wanted it to be nearly covered over.

Am I fooling myself? The *call* always sounds faintly because the part of man that seeks the truth sounds very faintly in ourselves. The impulse to search is also jammed in the middle of all our other interests and motivations. But it has a completely different quality. I wanted the people who came to wonder what it really was that brought them. I wanted them almost not to come. I am speaking, in short, about something young and uncertain in ourselves which wants to grow and become strong, but which is never nourished with the food proper to it, the food of ideas. Philosophy, art, science, religion exist all about us in our society. As they are, they do not bring the food I am speaking of. It is always wrapped or "cooked" in ways that this young part of our being cannot accept. We bring truths into ourselves wrapped in sex, personal ambition, romance, piety; spiced with fear or sentimentality, or else diluted by convention; or polluted by anger and impatience. Think how the influences of the great traditions of truth are brought to us: in sterile museums and classrooms, in smartly packaged books, in sanctimonious churches, in patterns of behavior which we alter to suit our pleasure and whim. In all of that, what becomes of the call sent out to humanity through great works of art, philosophy, science, religion—in ancient rites and customs and even manners whose origins lie in minds far greater than our own?

Was I fooling myself? Could I really begin this course with the proper "sound"?

I did not know whether to feel pleased or disturbed that so many parents came to the initial meeting. Our hostess's living room was overflowing—people sitting on the floor, crowding in doorways, spilling out into the dining room.

I began the evening by reading aloud a long excerpt from Leo Tolstoy's *My Confession*, in which the author describes how, at the age of fifty and at the height of his powers and success, he was gradually, but inexorably overcome "by minutes at first of perplexity and then of an arrest of life, as though I did not know how to live or what to do." These periods, writes Tolstoy, gradually became more frequent and always found their expression in the questions: "Why? Well, and then?"

The questions seemed foolish, simple, and childish.

"But the moment I touched them and tried to solve them, I became convinced in the first place that they were not childish and foolish, but very important and profound questions in life, and, in the second, that no matter how much I might try, I should not be able to answer them." What is the meaning of life? "Before attending to my Samára estate, to my son's education, or to the writing of a book, I ought to know why I should do that. So long as I did not know why, I could not do anything. I could not live."

He continues:

> Amidst my thoughts of farming, which interested me very much during that time, there would suddenly pass through my head a question like this: "All right, you are going to have six thousand desyatínas of land in the Government of Samára, and three hundred horses—and then?" And I completely lost my senses and did not know what to think further. Or, when I thought of the education of my children, I said to myself: "Why?" Or, reflecting on the manner in which the masses might obtain their welfare, I suddenly said to myself: "What is that to me?" Or, thinking of the fame which my works would get me, I said to myself: "All right, you will be more famous than Gógol, Púshkin, Shakespeare, Molière, and all the writers in the world— what of it?" And I was absolutely unable to make any reply. The questions were not waiting, and I had to answer them at once. If I did not answer them, I could not live.
>
> I felt that what I was standing on had given way, that I had no foundation to stand on, that that which I lived by no longer existed, and that I had nothing to live by.*

And this, Tolstoy continues, all took place at a period in his life when he had attained everything he had ever wanted, everything anyone could want. "I was on every side surrounded by what

---

*Leo Tolstoy, *My Confession*, trans. Leo Wiener (Boston: Colonial Press, 1904), pp. 17–18.

is considered to be complete happiness"—a good and loving wife, good children, wealth and property, fame and exceptional health and vigor. Yet, "in such condition I arrived at the conclusion that I could not live, and, fearing death, I had to use cunning against myself, in order that I might not take my life."

He then goes on to relate an ancient Eastern story to describe how he saw his own situation. As I read this story aloud to the parents, I observed them growing quieter and quieter. The people sitting uncomfortably on the floor stopped fidgeting, and even those standing against the wall became nearly motionless.

Long ago has been told the Eastern story about the traveller who in the steppe is overtaken by an infuriated beast. Trying to save himself from the animal, the traveller jumps into a waterless well, but at its bottom he sees a dragon who opens his jaws in order to swallow him. And the unfortunate man does not dare climb out, lest he perish from the infuriated beast, and does not dare jump down to the bottom of the well, lest he be devoured by the dragon, and so clutches the twig of a wild bush growing in a cleft of the well and holds on to it. His hands grow weak and he feels that soon he shall have to surrender to the peril which awaits him on either side; but he still holds on and sees two mice, one white, the other black, in even measure making a circle around the main trunk of the bush to which he is clinging, and nibbling at it on all sides. Now, at any moment, the bush will break and tear off, and he will fall into the dragon's jaws. The traveller sees that and knows that he will inevitably perish; but while he is still clinging, he sees some drops of honey hanging on the leaves of the bush, and so reaches out for them with his tongue and licks the leaves.*

*Ibid., pp. 21–22.

How still the room had become. It was incomprehensible. Could it be that everyone felt the same objective terror in front of the idea that all the so-called good things in life are only such "drops of honey"?

Why, they were even more attentive and rapt than their children! What was going on? I saw my theories, based on real observations, begin to crumble. I had expected to see less interest in these parents, less openness to ideas that challenge the basis of one's understanding of life. Having seen, after much work and over a reasonably extended period of time, that their adolescent children were not yet entirely cut off from the longing for ideas, I was certain I would encounter layer upon layer of resistance in the parents—of the sort I met at the first meeting in the school, and of the sort I knew only too well in all the people that one encounters over the course of one's day-to-day life. Yet here they were, even more concentrated than their children!

I quickly concluded the reading in order to launch the discussion. I began, as usual, with Plato. I decided not to mince words, but went right into the theory of Forms, the Platonic Ideas, Plato's central teaching about the being of all beings, his equation of being with *meaning*.

It was not until halfway through the evening, during the coffee break, that the truth of what was happening began to dawn on me, and when it did I experienced for the second time that evening two strong contradictory impressions at the same time. In this case, however, what I saw sent a shudder through me. My original theory about the difference between the parents and their children, which had just before seemed to be in jeopardy, was now reconfirmed. But my satisfaction at being on the right track after all was almost completely eclipsed by the sense of shock at what I saw in the parents and in myself.

What I had taken for attention and seriousness of purpose was nothing more than politeness! Respectful curiosity! I saw it in their questions and comments during the break—how ideas that both challenged their lives at the very root and opened up vast new worlds of value and purpose, how all of that had been captured in a tiny part of the mind and instantly tamed into some purring little kitten with unusual markings. There were no roaring tigers here.

Equally astonishing was the degree to which I myself had been taken in. I had lectured and moderated the discussion for over an hour utterly enmeshed in a fantasy about my audience. Realizing that, I felt a strangely familiar sense of relaxation pass over me as I sipped my coffee. I munched a cookie and lit a cigarette. I was one of them. It felt good. Was I not also a parent? Why should I not enjoy being the center of attention and admiration? Did I not have some important things to say to them? Was I not an eminent professor and author? After all . . . after all . . .

For almost all of the second hour I saw, with varying degrees of clarity, Professor Jacob Needleman.

The next meeting with the parents finally produced the real result I had been hoping for, but in such an unexpected way that I almost laughed out loud. Not because there was anything amusing about it but because what appeared was so simple and so profound at the same time. I now understand the real difference between an adult and an adolescent, but how can I communicate the importance and newness of this discovery?

At this meeting, the numbers were down to about twenty. In part, this was due to another notice sent out to the first group. asking for a commitment to attend the full series of lectures (four) and requesting a moderate amount of money for me. Also, that same night was the night of the annual school talent show, a major social event. Those who came to the meeting, therefore, were the parents who were interested enough to pay a little money and sacrifice attending the show.

Also present at the meeting was one of the children from the school, the absolutely charming daughter of the hosts for that evening. Her name was Beth and had I myself been a boy of seventeen I would have fallen in love with her immediately. As it was, I was a little bit disturbed that she was there, as my aim was to work only with the parents. Her presence, however, turned out to be of decisive importance.

I had assigned the group the first four books of the *Republic*. Here Socrates is asked, in effect, to prove that it is better for a man to be just and good no matter what other evils may befall him. At the outset, various definitions of justice are offered and immediately shown to be inconsistent and naive. The redoubtable Thrasymachus then enters the fray full of bluster and self-assurance, mocking Socrates' pretense of ignorance and the whole enterprise of serious philosophical inquiry itself. He cannot resist offering his own definition, to the effect that justice is nothing more than that which is in the interest of the strong; might is right; there is no objective justice or goodness in human life. Thus, even while mocking Socrates and philosophy, Thrasymachus falls into Socrates' net and is dispatched with a few well-aimed logical thrusts.

Book One of the *Republic* ends. It is clear that words alone, concepts alone, definitions, analysis cannot answer the question of justice and morality. Vision, not argument, is needed—a vision of the very structure of human nature and its place in the whole, universal world. The demand placed upon Socrates is severe and uncompromising. Do not give us hypotheses, Socrates, do not merely rearrange our opinions and definitions. Do not compel us with logic only, or inference, or so-called common sense. No, Socrates, show our hearts and minds together that it is better for a man to be just and good. Take the perfectly just man, cast him in prison, give him a reputation for evil, take away family, friends, wealth; put him in chains, on the rack, scourge him, burn out his eyes, crucify him. Against this, place a man who is evil and unjust down to his very bones—but let him be thought by all to be good and just; give him wealth, honor, power, and everything else the world calls good. Now, Socrates, show us that the first is happier than the second, that no matter what, it is better to be, rather than only to seem, just and good. Make us understand that the good of human life is to be measured by a man's inner being, by the state of his soul and by nothing else!

Socrates accepts the challenge. There now begins the unfolding of one of the most powerful and precise metaphors of human life in all the literature of the world. Let us first envision a city that is just, says Socrates, a government of men and women that we shall construct from zero. Only then, when we have seen the being of man writ large, will we see what justice means within the individual, within each of ourselves.

Immediately, a principle is discovered—deceptively simple in appearance—that is to generate the entire dynamism of the inner and outer "republic" of man: *Each man must do the work to which he is suited by nature*—the farmer, the carpenter, the smith. But when this principle is established, there all too quickly appears the apparent solution to the question—a solution that destroys itself the moment it is put forward. An ideal city appears that Socrates ironically labels "healthy": a small community of men and women living off the land, growing their own food, living in simple huts, eating and sleeping and singing.

Healthy? You have shown us a city fit for pigs, not men, says Glaucon. It is true, even though Glaucon does not realize how true. Man is more than his healthy appetites, his material nature, far more. In order to establish a city that reflects everything about man, including every refined and even luxuriant desire—in order for a presiding justice to appear that can harmonize the whole reach of the human entity, more land is needed, and for that— trade and *war*, that is to say, struggle, effort, risk, danger—engagement with other cities and peoples.

Now, and only now, must there appear within the city a new kind of force, a new sort of man—who cares for the good of the *whole*, and not only for this or that aspect of the whole. Not farmers who care for the crops, not carpenters who care for the shelter, not smiths who forge the metals, but a man who attends to the needs and nature of the whole community together, who knows what is good and what is bad, and who is moreover able to struggle for it, defending the city against its enemies and welcoming its friends.

This force in man that understands and cares for the whole is represented by the *guardians*. They are a breed apart. The guardian is a lover of learning and wisdom, not a lover of food or possessions or sexual pleasure or security—as are the tradesmen and artisans. He has the will, the special emotional energy called *thumos*, to overcome every obstacle or "enemy" in the service of this love; he is a warrior.

Thumos is a term exceedingly difficult to translate into contemporary language. The best that scholars have been able to do is to apply the word "spirit," in the sense that one speaks of a "spirited" horse, a "spirited" fighter. It is a force of striving and overcoming. It is not simply another desire; it is a unique quality of energy. When guided by wisdom and understanding, it is *will*; when guided by the appetites, it is obsession or even madness.

> Then he who is to be a really good and noble guardian of the State will require to unite in himself philosophy and spirit and swiftness and strength?
> Undoubtedly.
> Then we have found the desired natures (to rule the State); and now that we have them, how are they to be reared and educated?*

The education of the guardians: If the real theme of the *Republic* is the nature of man, this is the theme within the theme. How to identify the guardian nature within man, how to support it,

---

*Plato, *Republic* 376B, *The Dialogues of Plato*, 4th ed., trans. Benjamin Jowett (Oxford University Press, 1953).

nourish it, test it, bring it to its rightful place as ruler within the flowing structure of human life, my own human life here and now?

As the last of the parents took their places, I reached into my briefcase for my copy of the text and, trying to be as nonsociable as possible, I asked everyone to turn to Book I. I was not surprised to see a dozen sheepish looks on people's faces. For the next fifteen minutes or so, I was presiding over a sort of mass confessional. "I tried to read it," said one man, "I even kept it by my bed."

"I found the language too old-fashioned," said another.

"I just kept putting it off."

"It made me sleepy."

"I started reading it and then got hooked by another book."

And so on.

I smiled to myself. It was very good, this. I didn't know why, exactly, but I felt something very right about the fact that so many were unable to do the assignment and yet were willing to come back. Professorially, I should have been irritated or disappointed, I suppose. But I wasn't trying anything professorial with these grown-up men and women all in the midst of busy successful lives which, at the same time, concealed a gaping vacuum, as do almost all our lives.

"I want to get right to the heart of the matter," I said, dismissing the whole issue of doing or not doing the assignment. "I want to read you a passage from the *Republic* that states the entire message of Plato in a few words. But I warn you, when you hear this passage you will not feel its immense significance. Only later, after you have broken your heads trying to understand this book and the ideas in it, will you begin to sense the revolutionary power of what I'm about to read to you."

I turned to the end of Book IV and read aloud:

> But in reality justice was such as we were describing, being concerned however, not with the outward man, but

with the inward, which is the true self and the true concern of man; for the just man does not permit the several elements within him to interfere with one another, or any of them to do the work of others—he sets in order his own inner life, and is his own master and his own law, in unison with himself; and when he has bound together the three principles within him, which may be compared to the higher, lower and middle notes of the scale, and the intermediate intervals—when he has bound all these together, and is no longer many, but has become one entirely temperate and perfectly adjusted nature, then he proceeds to act, if he has to act, whether in a matter of property, or in the treatment of the body, or in some other affair of politics or private business; always thinking and calling that which preserves and co-operates with this harmonious condition, just and good actions, and the knowledge which presides over it, wisdom, and that which at any time impairs this condition, he will call unjust action, and the opinion which presides over it, ignorance. *

It was exactly as I expected and foretold: polite interest—no feeling. "The *Republic*," I said, "is about man considered as three-storied structure, a tripartite being. All the sufferings and evils of human life arise because these three parts are out of relationship to each other. The aim of human life is, first, to bring these parts back together and then to manifest that harmony in one's life with one's fellow man."

And then I said: "There you have it. That is the whole message of Plato. If you want your money back, now is the time to say so, because the rest of our time together will be spent only explaining what this means."

General laughter, sipping of coffee, lighting of cigarettes. Ex-

Republic, 444d–3, adapted from Jowett translation.

cept for Beth, the hosts' teenage daughter. Her beautiful, wide-open face was burning with interest.

I then proceeded to summarize the first books of the *Republic* in the light of the doctrine of the three parts of human nature, *logistikon*, *thumos*, and *epithumia*, the intellectual function, the function of the striving spirit, and the function of attractions, fears, desires, and appetites. I emphasized the other basic division of the self for Plato, the division of two fundamental movements within man, the movement toward Being and the movement toward outer things and appearances. However, I did little more than touch on Plato's full characterization of the intellect as *nous*, the harmonizing presence and consciousness within man that at the same time experiences and understands the universal world directly.

Throughout this presentation, questions were sporadic and superficial—again, except for Beth, who, it was clear, was following everything all the way. I even detected in her a trace of pity for the adults who seemed to be having so much difficulty relating to the teachings of Plato. Beth and I soon began to exchange little glances of mutual understanding. I didn't like that.

I began to wish I was with my teenagers, where there was, comparatively speaking, such openness to philosophical questioning. I didn't like that, either. The sense of weight in this room, the human texture, the atmosphere—I didn't know what to call it—was completely different: richer and poorer at the same time, both more and less real, more and less serious at the same time.

I continued with my summary of the first half of the *Republic*. I was now entering the subject of the education of the guardians. It was here that the whole meaning of my work with the parents became clear to me.

It was in the middle of my discussion of the role of art in the development of man. I knew, of course, that this aspect of Plato's philosophy was difficult for most modern people to understand. We must, says Socrates, carefully regulate the sort of art that is allowed in our city. The proper education of the guardians—

which means the proper development of man—depends heavily on the influence of art, especially music and story. The State, therefore, can allow only a specific kind of art; all others must be banned.

One could practically hear hackles rising throughout the room.

"Censorship," said someone, drily. I fully expected that reaction. Most modern people who study Plato, including many scholars, balk at his views on art. He is almost universally condemned as an enemy of free artistic expression and for seeking to make art into mere propaganda that serves class interests and stifles dissent. Later on in the *Republic*, when Socrates evaluates types of political organization, the impression of Plato as totalitarian seems inescapable—especially when he unashamedly denigrates democracy. Even scholars who generally admire Platonic philosophy often find these aspects of his teachings offensive.

Of course, anyone who has lived in the twentieth century and has witnessed the horrors inflicted on mankind through totalitarianism and paranoiac political repression can hardly be blamed for misreading Plato in this way. Nevertheless, a misreading it remains. What is forgotten, and it is always the first thing forgotten, is that the *Republic* is a metaphor about the inner structure of man: myself. This single fact puts everything in a different light. Where Plato speaks of the rule of the guardians, he is speaking of the development of a ruling presence within the self. Where he speaks of the strength and courage of the warriors, he is speaking of a specific inner energy that obeys and struggles to execute the vision of truth; in a word, will. And where he speaks of the laborers, artisans, and merchants, he is speaking of the multitude of desires and appetites within oneself that can voluntarily submit to the goodness, wisdom, and striving of the higher centers of perception and action within human nature.

So I was not surprised at the murmurings about censorship. What did surprise me were people's reactions on the subject of art as such, even apart from the question of censorship. I did not realize, or else I had forgotten, the passion with which people hold views about art and the artist.

It was not hard for everyone to agree that art in general is directed principally to the emotional function in man. The question of the role of art in education is therefore a question of evoking emotions of a specific kind in the developing human being. It is the question of what sort of nourishment is best for the emotional component of the human psyche.

I proceeded very slowly, already sensing difficulties gathering in people's minds.

"Consider," I said, "how many of our patterns of feeling are adopted quite automatically when we are young, simply out of imitation. Think of the movies we saw when we were young. What emotions did they encourage in us? How many of us fell in love mainly because we saw it in the movies or read about it?"

"But you can't call that sort of thing art!" said Georgiana W., tilting forward on the couch opposite me, her graceful hand clutching the jeweled pendant that hung from her neck. Mrs. W.'s husband, seated next to her, was a prominent architect. He nodded brusquely in agreement with her.

"Of course it's art," said Herb S., from a chair behind her. "Art isn't just paintings hanging on a wall or in a museum. Art is everywhere."

That was exactly the point I wanted to make, and so I proceeded: "Isn't it obvious, when you think of it, that we're surrounded on all sides by art? Movies, TV, novels, the stories we're always reading. And music—music is everywhere, not just in concert halls; we're always hearing music—in stores, elevators, doctor's offices, in the car. And what about the things we handle every day? Somebody designed them in this or that way, didn't they? The houses we live in, the furniture we use, the clothes we wear . . ."

I stopped in midsentence to allow Beth to speak; she was bursting to say something. "Do we have any emotions that are our own?" she asked. My God, she was so far ahead of the discussion that, for the moment, I simply had to defer that point. "We'll come to that," I said. "First, I want to be sure we see the main significance of Plato's view of art.

"Art, says Plato, has immense power in human life, but especially when we are young or when anything in us is young and growing. It has the power to fix patterns of feeling and emotion in man. Can anyone deny that this is the most important aspect of education in its real meaning? If we are speaking of the moral development of man, surely we are speaking about the development of his emotional nature, since values that are not felt are not values at all—they have no power in our lives.

"Then we need to ask ourselves: What sorts of emotions are evoked and supported by the art that ordinarily surrounds us? At the same time, we also need to ask: Are there certain emotions which we consider less desirable than others? Obviously, there are. Who among us has a good word to say for hatred, self-pity, sentimentality, or fear? Yet most of the art we know trades in precisely these emotions."

I continued by suggesting that everyone try an experiment before the next meeting. It was the sort of simple experiment I had already suggested to my students at the high school, and which I have often tried at the university. It always clarifies Plato's views of art better than any explanation ever could. It is also a sort of time bomb that can go off right in your face. This time, merely speaking about it to the parents caused it to explode—although softly.

"As an experiment," I said, "try to notice the emotions that are evoked in you this week, at the theater or the movies or in front of the TV or at a concert or listening to recorded music—in front of any form of art you come in contact with. Just try to observe and take note of your emotional reactions. Don't pay too much attention to the subject matter, just observe your emotions if you can, and if you can remember to try.

"I think you will find this experiment very revealing. But you will need to separate some of your attention from the subject matter. It can be a play about some very lofty moral theme, but you will find, if I am not mistaken, that the actual emotions evoked in you are the sort we have just mentioned—self-pity, anger, self-righteousness, the craving for vengeance or something similar. Try. When you are gripped with suspense, try to look at yourself sincerely—you will see a person eagerly awaiting someone's violent death or some sentimental event that could not possibly take place in any universe, real or ideal."

Generally, people who try this experiment are surprised not so much by the emotions they see, but by how difficult it is to know what emotion they are in fact experiencing in front of art. This discovery is quite enough to bring home Plato's point about the unrecognized influence of art and to start people thinking about the sea of emotional influences we swim in, and in which our children swim.

When I have tried this experiment at the university, I have usually begun with a practical demonstration making use of recorded music. I take six or seven different kinds of music and play them to the class without telling them in advance what each is. I ask them only to try to notice what each evokes in them. For example, I recently tried this using sections of the following: a Sufi recitation on a reed pipe; a Gregorian chant; the fourth movement of Beethoven's Seventh Symphony; the first movement of the Tchaikovsky violin concerto; a popular "love ballad" of the 1940s era; a Country-and-Western song; and a Hard-Rock selection.

Here, too, of course, the attempt was more to dramatize an idea than to convey a real experience since, even in the relatively quiet and concentrated atmosphere of a college classroom, it is nearly impossible to be attentive enough to one's own emotions in front of art. This requires far more intensive conditions both in the listener and in the group as a whole than are to be found in any university class. Nevertheless, the experiment was effective at its own level. After playing the Sufi piece (which was actually also an inner exercise of the breath), I immediately played the Country-and-Western selection. Students were astonished to see the sharp sexual desire this music evoked in them, fueling, in this case, the emotion of self-pity suggested by the lyrics. Some people were even shocked by what they noticed in themselves after hearing the Beethoven selection—one student characterized it as a "pleasurable drugged sensation." Many, many observations of this kind were forthcoming. This experiment, even conducted at this relatively low level of precision, never fails to drive home the seriousness of Plato's idea of art as a formative influence on the emotional development of man.

As I was describing to the parents the sort of thing to look for when trying the experiment, I noticed that Mrs. W.'s face was growing dark. She was still leaning forward, holding onto her pendant, but her eyes were now cast down and she was frowning.

From the conversation that followed, it became clear that Mrs. W. and many others there had devoted much of their lives to the appreciation of art—in her case, music, about which she spoke very knowledgeably. In other words, she had acquired a great deal of material about music in her life and it meant quite a bit to her.

For a brief period, the atmosphere of politeness and respect for me, which enabled me more or less to say anything without being challenged, wore thin.

The soft explosion had begun.

Why do I give it such a dramatic name—"explosion"? Am I exaggerating just for effect? Not at all, although it is difficult to convey in words what was taking place at that moment. Remember: Here I am, a professor of philosophy, an author, what the world calls "a distinguished scholar." In short, I am an "authority." The people with whom I am speaking have unbounded respect for such a figure, although, and perhaps because, their adult lives have taken them away from the atmosphere of the university. Remember, too, that they have invited me into their homes, that all this is proceeding in the most gracious and genteel of surroundings. And remember that the subject matter is philosophy, Plato—not the sort of subject one is predisposed to fight about—not politics or some topic of pressing social concern, like nuclear energy, say, or the abortion issue. The people here have quite sincerely come to learn, not to argue; to make contact with a world they feel they have grown too far away from—the world of ideas and study. Finally, remember the atmosphere of warmth and fine manners, bordering on a semiformal social occasion among friends where the last thing one expects is to have a knife inserted into one's feelings about one's own life.

You are a busy, successful person; you are holding together a family and a good career; you are raising children in the best way you know how; you have kept up your mind and your sensibilities with respect to the finer things of life—the arts in particular, music, painting, literature; you read, haphazardly to be sure, good books, serious things, as much as you can. You have built up a store of ideas and information, much of it based on long personal experience, and so you are not without intellectual tools which you have honed, also haphazardly, by discussion when and where the occasion has presented itself. You have logic, you have some thoughts, you have a store of material that you have gathered about life. And you have brought that all with you in order to learn something new, to broaden your interests and your understanding. You are an adult. You are not an adolescent.

Now, you have been following, with interest, the development of a system of ideas that is fascinating, difficult, challenging—one that throws into question many of your assumptions and that brings whole new perspectives about the structure of man and the universe itself. You let it in, gradually, carefully, and—to some extent—you are able to meet it with the material you have gathered about life. Being new, these ideas are external to you; you wish to meet them and balance them with your own feelings and values. They are out there; you are in here. Exciting, interesting, they are all that you hoped for from philosophy; something to make you think again about everything, something you have missed in your life. How good, how necessary this is to being a real person.

I know you: You are me; it is how we all face great ideas when we are at our serious best. You find some things difficult to swallow and it is amazing that this young girl, Beth or whoever it happens to be, grasps it all so quickly and accepts it all. She is so young, how is it that she is so open, when you and I are having such difficulty? In fact, it is annoying.

But now something is happening to you that does not happen to Beth or to any adolescent. You have all this material you have gathered about life; she has none, or very little—and what little she may have is not yet firmly secured to her personality. (To the extent that it is firmly secured, she is already an adult.) She is more open to great ideas than you, far more open (and we need to know that about our children; it is vital that we know it). *But it costs her nothing*. With you, parent, it is different. It costs you a great deal when an idea suddenly penetrates behind all your material, all your experience, all your knowledge, and is now no longer external to you. This idea about art and human emotion, for example, is not something you can meet. Quite the contrary: *In front of this idea, you meet yourself*.

Does this explain at all what I mean by the word "explosion"? When Mrs. W. leaned back against the couch there was neither light nor darkness in her face. Every furrow had disappeared from her forehead and her eyes were quiet and luminous, not darting back and forth looking for thoughts. What were those eyes seeing? Her hands, no longer clutching the pendant, rested gracefully in her lap.

What more can I say? The idea of *remembering* has been used not only by Socrates and Pythagoras, but by all the great teachers of truth of all epochs. If it has any meaning at all, it must, I am certain, start from that extraordinary state of presence that Mrs. W. was then experiencing.

Can anything be called philosophy—the love of wisdom, the love of being—that does not guide us toward that state and remind us of it throughout the conduct of our lives? What deeper, more authentically human search begins from this moment when an original, deeply internal love—the love of art or beauty or science or God or my neighbor—is allowed to separate from everything in us that has dressed it up in fashionable clothes? Remembering begins from just this condition of internal division along the ontologically fundamental lines of human nature: on the one hand, the primal, original impulse toward being; and on the other hand, the numerous psychological functions and faculties that are designed to deal with the material world around us.

And if one asks: What, then, is remembered? the answer can only be: my Self.

PART III

Remembering
Philosophy

CHAPTER 8

Eros and Ego: Toward a Redefinition of the History of Philosophy

There are two stages in the study of philosophy corresponding to two principal stages of human life itself. At the beginning, the purpose of philosophy is to bring the mind back again and again to the need to see the world as though from another level, another dimension, that gives everything in front of us a different cast and value. This is a power of the mind that points us toward a higher level of being within human nature. It is not yet the higher level itself. It is adolescent, in between the unformed openness of the child and the formed individual ego of the adult. It is an orientation of the mind, a feeling in the mind—that same mind which is also being shaped and limited on all sides by the pragmatic needs and influences of the everyday world with its psychological and physical survival values, its material and its social exigencies.

The second stage occurs when great ideas conduct us toward a direct encounter between this feeling in the mind, this love of truth on the one hand, and on the other hand the formed individual ego itself with its specific desires and fears, the deeply ingrained opinions that support them and, most importantly, the knowledge gained, the tastes formed, and even the philosophical views reached in that part of the psyche which is generally understood to be the adult human personality. The second stage of philosophy corresponds to that stage of human development, not reached by everyone in their lives, in which it is seen that all one's material, all one's data—scientific, ethical, religious, artistic—have been acquired in a small part of oneself and have been fatally shaped and locked in that part where they serve only social and survival values such as the desire for recognition, safety, physical health, fame; identification with one's country, race, or social group; the desire for pleasure and satisfaction; the craving for tidiness in explanations or personal life. The second stage is the confrontation between the love of being and the mind of the ego. These two parts of human nature are experienced as utterly incommensurate and express themselves in completely opposed sets of values. To bring an individual to this confrontation is the ultimate purpose of the philosophical study of great ideas; beyond that confrontation quite a different kind of study is necessary. This second stage is not for children.

It is possible to regard the entire history of ideas in our civilization from the perspective of this distinction. Under the influence of the first stage of philosophy, man conceives of the world about him, the world revealed to his senses in space and time, as a tissue of appearances, more or less illusory. Beyond this world, inaccessible to ordinary knowledge and perception, lies another world, the real world of things in themselves; and the world we live in is at best a shadow, a reflection, of the real world. This idea, in many and varied forms, is the principal governing idea in the history of philosophy. Under one guise or another, its expression and development stretches from the teachings of Pythagoras through Socrates and Plato, Aristotle, the medieval epoch, the Renaissance, and the modern era. Today, as in earliest antiquity, it has the power to touch some extraordinary chord in man's mind. What is it in ourselves that responds to this idea? Surely it is something, some impulse, which itself lies behind the phenomena of our own psychological world—our ordinary thoughts, opinions, desires, and motivations. It has been named *eros* and symbolized in an image of "adolescence," a youthful spirit between mortal man and the immortal gods.

Ultimately, however, all those who pursue the first stage of philosophy with serious intent discover that the world of appearances, the "illusory" world in which we live our lives, has a stubborn reality to it. It refuses to dissolve, to step back; it insists itself, it must be dealt with, lived in, organized. It makes imperious claims upon our energy and attention, never shaping itself into the ideal forms of the metaphysical world. The world we live in, in fact, contradicts the ideal reality toward which we are drawn by *eros*, and this contradiction remains inescapable as long as we live. How will we face this contradiction?

It is the same within ourselves. Our own thoughts, emotions, and physical habits continuously form themselves into the identity of ego which continuously opposes the wish for inner being, freedom of consciousness, and moral power. How will we face this contradiction within ourselves?

Great ideas have lost their power in our civilization and in our lives because man has tried to pass directly from the first stage of philosophy into practical action without being led into the second stage. That is to say, he has sought to move from a vision of higher truth to moral action without confronting long enough or deeply enough the contradiction between the movement toward unity and the movement toward dispersal in all spheres of existence, but especially within himself. He has tried to go directly from adolescence to perfection without living in front of his own two natures, the god and the animal within him.

The confrontation I am speaking of may seem like a small thing compared to the great ideas and teachings that have been handed down through the centuries. Mrs. W., casting her eyes down and suffering the struggle between all her ordinary knowledge and the sudden awareness of an idea that moves her heart in another direction: Do I really mean to place that momentary experience above the great ideas themselves? In fact, that is precisely what I mean. However, whether Mrs. W. ever comes back to that moment and whether she draws the correct conclusions from it, is quite another matter. What I am claiming is that in such an experience, philosophy has taken her as far as it can take any human being. Beyond this point, ideas need to be associated with a specific inner struggle over a long period of time.

The encounter between the wish for being and the mind of the ego may be identified as the single most important transitional moment in the life of any grown-up man or woman. This is something which must be faced in front of all the great problems of living. Behind the problem, lies the Question. Through this encounter, if it is persistent and deep enough, a new mind arises in man which Plato identified as *nous*, the higher consciousness, which can apprehend the world as it is in itself. This new mind, this new Self, is nourished only through prolonged struggle between the two natures—that is to say, only through a prolonged facing of the Question in myself.

However, we are moving too fast. Before this decisive encounter between the two natures can take place, there must first appear the search for truth, the ignition of *eros* in the ordinary intellect and feelings of man. Philosophical ideas about the whole of human life and the cosmos must circulate in the human environment as an influence that can attract and magnetize the ordinary mind.

These ideas exist—in abundance. Not only Plato has injected such ideas into the stream of Western civilization, although the influence of Platonic ideas has doubtless been the most important in our history. The "children" and "grandchildren" of Plato—from Aristotle to the Neoplatonists and beyond—have contributed their own massive portion of philosophical formulations to the life of Western man. Here, too, we must also list the Stoics with their powerful notions of inner and outer universal mind, their binding together of the rules of ethics and the transformation of the human psychological structure. Then, too, there are the vast worlds of

Judaic and Christian philosophy—Maimonides, Augustine, Scotus Erigena, Aquinas, and countless others. And, coming later, there is Spinoza's vision of reality "under the aspect of eternity"; there is Immanuel Kant's revolutionary formulation of the idea of the noumenon; there is Hegel's vision of Mind moving in the great sweep of historical time.

The point now is not to list these many channels by which universal ideas have entered the general turnover of Western life—we shall look at some of these currents of thought presently. The point is to recognize that there have always existed ideas that can lead us to regard our lives from the perspective of another scale of reality. At the same time, however, the action of these ideas has become progressively blocked in the twentieth century. Philosophy as an influence orienting man to another reality within and outside of himself has nearly vanished from our culture. It is time to bring it back.

I say "bring it back," but that is not a very precise expression. The point is that it is coming back by its own power. The real question is whether we will be open to it as such. The great ideas created in the initiatic centers of antiquity continue to exist and are now entering the culture in new ways, new formulations, new expressions. Through whom and through what are they entering?

Before answering that question, we must also note that it is not only the intellectual formulation of great ideas that are once again mixing with the social and survival influences of the contemporary world. Philosophical ideas are but one of the forms by which awakening teachings send out their signatures into the turnover of everyday life, the life of war and peace, health and illness, family and government, the life in which men struggle and yearn for fame, sex, safety, romance, adventure, amusement, the life in which they fight and retreat, protect and destroy one another—the world of *maya*, *samsara*, the world and life characterized by Ecclesiastes by the words "vanity, vanity." Our world.

As from some mythic central source above and within the

world of vanity "under the sun," there appear in all times and cultures signposts of another direction, another meaning to the whole of life. Philosophical ideas, forms of art, architecture, music, symbol, rites and customs, rituals, legends, scriptures, modes of dance and teachings about the human body, psychological and ethical rules—all this and much else besides can come from these mythic/actual centers of knowledge into the very atmosphere in which men conduct their lives. In this world of everyday life they mix with the influences of the ordinary mind, the social and survival forces of the world, and gradually lose their purity and awakening power. Then they may separate out again, regaining something of their clarity—or new sources of such influences may suddenly appear, sending out once more in new form their awakening influences—new philosophical formulations of the indestructible truths, or new art, new symbols, new myths and scripture superficially different from the ancient signposts, but in fact containing the power to call men back once again to the great search. By means of such signposts, the individual is brought to the threshold of the subjective encounter between the love of truth and the system of the ego, at which point a quite different sort of influence is necessary, one that cannot be given through anything less than direct, personal training in total self-interrogation and guidance in sensitivity to the state of remembering.

I am asserting that the primary function of philosophy is to inject into the mind of man an influence of a very special kind. By helping an individual to think about life and the world from the perspective of a greater scale of reality, it points him toward something, he knows not what, behind the world of appearances in which he is caught from the moment he is born to the moment of his death. At the same time, it points him to something in himself, he knows not what, that is more real than the personal identity which his social environment has thrust upon him—a certain feeling for truth, a certain love or yearning that is the embryo of something very great in him. In its second stage, philosophy brings man to the realization that this embryonic immensity within him is opposed by his personal ego and that out there, in the external world, there are also two great forces inherently opposed to each other. It is this realization of the twoness of himself and the world which man needs to "digest," impartially and over a long period of time under "Socrates," that is, under an entirely different kind of influence. Through the guidance and influence of "Socrates," inner work leading to transformation begins and the strictly philosophical study of ideas ceases. The embryo is nourished by philosophy, but the child is delivered by "Socrates" and grows under "his" parentage.

In short, the principal task of philosophy is to bring something new into the wretched sleep of man, to trouble that sleep with a great and tremendous dream that finally stirs a man into an instant of awakening. Across the room, in the dim obscurity of night, he sees a figure standing quietly. It is Socrates, and behind Socrates stands another figure, impossible to discern, but strangely familiar. It is himself.

It remains, then, to begin the work of redefining the history of philosophical ideas for our time. It is necessary to bring philosophy back to its proper role as a call to remembering.

CHAPTER 9

Reality: The Problem and the Question

I was eleven years old when the atomic bomb was dropped on Hiroshima. I remember the thick headlines and the photograph of the mushroom cloud covering the whole front page of the newspaper. I remember feeling: *Something new has entered our lives.* I felt this instantly, without even being entirely sure what the word "atomic" meant. I opened the paper and quickly closed it. For some reason, I didn't want to read anything about it.

The whole day at school the photograph haunted me. There was much talk about the bomb even during recess, but I was tuning out from all that. *The war would soon be over:* Yes, that was wonderful. A new, unlimited source of energy had been discovered: yes, I supposed, that also was good, whatever it was. "Enough energy in a single pebble to run an entire city"—that caught me a bit more, and I remember picking up a small stone and looking at it wonderingly. Yet, without too much surprise. That material things were full of immense energy was no more astonishing than the fact that things existed at all. One or two classmates said something about the immorality of the bomb, but no one paid attention to them. The most vociferous was Howie Weiss, a skinny, bespectacled boy who was always prattling about capitalism or the proletariat.

I kept back from all the talk. I was waiting impatiently for the school day to end so that I could discuss the whole thing with Elias Barkhordian.

Elias Barkhordian was a year older than I and tall for his age, heavy, with a big, round face and brilliant, dark eyes. I can see him now turning the corner of Franklin Street and ambling slowly toward me. Every afternoon I would be waiting for him at the low stone wall that surrounded our neighbor's lawn, away from the noise and excitement of the street games that began every day after school and continued on until after dark.

Elias lived only two blocks from our street, but in our neighborhood that was a great distance, especially as Elias went to a different school, a private school of some kind, and lived in what to us seemed a big, impressive house. He never joined in any of the games and was considered a sort of freak and a snob by the other neighborhood kids. My friendship with him was also considered suspect.

I don't remember when we discovered that we each wanted to talk about philosophical questions, but it was an utterly natural discovery for us. Our conversations would drift all by themselves in certain directions and a particular feeling would start building up in us. I do remember the time it occurred to him to ask who created God—I remember staring at his great, smooth forehead as though I was trying to look into his brain. I realized that when he asked that question he was not merely challenging me, but challenging the whole universe. It was the first philosophical question I ever experienced. It sent an extraordinary feeling of freedom through me. And I remember saying to myself the words, *This is my best friend*.

I should mention one little ritual that preceded our talks. As he came toward me, he would gradually slow his pace practically to a standstill. This was the cue for me to walk toward him and be the first to speak. We would always pretend to be surprised to see each other, and I had to be the one to suggest we sit down on the wall, which we did even when it was covered with ice and snow. An element of formality, unusual for children these days, characterized our friendship throughout the year and a half that I knew him. He died of leukemia just before his fourteenth birthday.

I always called him "Elias," not "Eli."

That afternoon I had brought the newspaper with me. I could not conceal my excitement. But what exactly was I excited about?

"Isn't it tremendous?" I said.

Elias quite placidly proceeded to reel off, in that high and strangely even voice of his, the whole of the atomic theory, which he had probably just boned up on in the encyclopedia that afternoon. In order not to appear stupid, I responded by reciting a bunch of facts I happened to know about the sun and the solar system—sizes, distances, temperatures, and anything else I could recall from my voracious readings of astronomy books.

Elias countered with more facts about atoms, electrons, protons, molecules. I came back again with stars and galaxies and a few choice items about the rings of Saturn.

Our conversation was proceeding according to its customary pattern. We would always begin with this sort of competitive chatter, sometimes with amusement, sometimes argumentatively. But sooner or later, without fail, some thought or idea would appear that brought us to a halt. Down deep, we both knew that was what we were groping for. This time, it came out of Elias's mouth: "Maybe," he said, "the earth is an electron."

After a long pause during which we both savored the thought, I said: "And we're living inside of an atom."

"The sun is the nucleus," said Elias.

"And the stars, the galaxies . . ."

"Other atoms, molecules, cells," he went on, "in some gigantic organism."

We both fell silent.

We remained sitting there without speaking for a long time. Elias stared at the sky, his arms crossed in front of him. I was hunched over, looking intently at the ground, my elbows supported on my knees and my head cupped in my hands. I watched some ants crawling around my shoe. I thought to myself: We human beings are just like those ants. Absently, I stepped on the ants, but when I moved my foot away they were all still crawling around as though nothing had happened.

"How far down does it go?" I wondered aloud, picking up one of the ants.

Still gazing at the sky, Elias answered: "Maybe it goes on forever, worlds inside of worlds inside of worlds."

"It can't," I said. "It has to stop somewhere." I watched the ant crawling excitedly over the back of my hand, stopping at each hair as though it were a tree.

Maybe Elias was right, I thought. Maybe it does go down forever and ever, and maybe it goes up forever and ever, bigger and bigger worlds, stars, galaxies, universes, superuniverses—and it's all inside me and inside this ant and everything else. To my surprise, I felt tears coming to my eyes.

At just that moment I picked the ant up between the thumb and forefinger of my other hand and squashed it. A sensation like a small jolt of electricity shot through me. Killing the ant made me feel connected with life, with nature.

Behind the problem of ecology lies the question of man's relationship to nature. The question of man's relationship to nature is identical to the question of man's relationship to reality itself. Nature is reality. But "How far down does it go?" "How far up does it go?" Who has not felt this question at one time or another in his life? Why does it haunt the mind for so many of us, sometimes throughout the whole of our lives?

When I began to study philosophy more or less formally, even the word "ecology" was unknown. Nature was still generally felt to be a surrounding sea of reality, infinitely vast, infinitely powerful. Science, even though it had long since taken on a dominant life of its own in our culture, could still be regarded as an attempt to understand nature and not just manipulate it. Its theories and discoveries could still be taken as material for pondering the sort of question a child asks himself looking up at the sky. One was quite willing to make a detour through the difficult study of mathematics, physics, and chemistry, firm in the belief that something might lie at the end of such studies that would be crucially important to the solution of such deeply felt questions. One didn't have to be told anything about man's responsibilities to nature, or "stewarding the earth," or anything of the sort. And why? Because the burning desire to know the truth about reality was itself a moral force. That desire, that love of truth for its own sake, would not destroy or kill or injure or despoil. Of course, it is true that the problems associated with technology's effects on the environment had not yet called attention to themselves. This was in part because one was studying reality, not some limited aspect of it called "the environment." How could reality ever be endangered?

Up until quite recently, therefore, the idea of nature as reality, as God, still had an action, an influence in our culture. One could say that at its root science did not deny the Judeo-Christian idea of God; rather, it substituted another word for it: nature. Or, putting the matter differently, one could say that it sought to study an aspect of God that the Church had neglected: His operation in the external world. The Church taught about the inner demands that God made upon man; science taught about the way God worked. Behind both was the idea of man's existence within an all-encompassing reality beyond the immediate appearances. This all-encompassing reality obliged man to find his real relationship to it—either through the function of knowing (science) or the function of feeling (religious faith).

But environment is not nature, understood as an all-encompassing reality within which the whole life of mankind is but one element, or one level. The environment is only that part of nature or reality which man sees as necessary to his physical survival. The environment is modern technological man's word for "world," reality, nature. One cannot stand in wonder in front of the environment, one can only worry. When man worries, he turns for help to thoughts, theories, and concepts. Thus the great idea of nature, falling completely under the sway of fear, becomes a theoretical construct, a concept, a mental instrument in the service of physical and social needs. To bring back the awakening force of the great idea of nature, it is necessary to *remember* what the real and complete environment of man is. Environment is not greater and higher than man; nature is. Environment does not call to something within the human mind that is more real than the system of the ego; nature does.

Speaking historically, one could say that modern philosophy begins by offering the idea of nature as another name for God—that is to say, its aim is to prove that science and Christianity are speaking about the same thing. The great philosophers of the modern era—Descartes, Spinoza, Hume, Kant, Leibniz, Hegel—along with the fathers of modern science—Copernicus, Galileo, Newton, Kepler—are channels through which the idea of nature was redefined as an influence on the heart of man comparable to the fundamental message of religion.

Each of these philosophers uses the scientific model of thought—argument, logic, comparison, observation—rather than the mythic model, in order to express the idea of nature as another level of reality within which mankind lives and moves. For Descartes (1596–1650), this higher level of reality is a mathematically ordered whole created and maintained by the will of the absolute God. In order for man to situate himself and his life in a proper relationship to this fundamental reality, he must free his mind from the influence of his sensory and emotional automatisms.

Descartes is famous for his dictum, *I think, therefore I am.* Searching for a kind of knowing that nothing could overthrow, Descartes realized that the only thing he could be absolutely certain of was his own existence in the very experience of inquiry. Even if everything else he believed and thought about was false, so he reasoned, something that believes and thinks must necessarily exist. I can doubt everything—except the fact of doubting itself, the fact that I am indeed doubting at that very moment.

A small thing, perhaps, yet to Descartes it was an immense

discovery. He found a standard of certainty, a very high standard, and he vowed to believe only that which had the same quality of indubitable certainty. Upon this basis he now moves out to examine all the other ideas in his mind. Chief among them is the idea of God.

Descartes has found his standard of certainty—but, he asks, suppose reality were ordered in such a way that the experience of certainty, clarity, and distinctness was not really reliable. Suppose the creator of the world was a malicious trickster. If that were so, no man could ever get beyond the single, simple truth of "I think, therefore I am" (because even if there were a malicious God tricking me, I could still be certain that I exist if only as someone who was being tricked). Descartes wants more than this single, barren truth—obviously. He wants to know the whole order of reality, the structure of nature itself.

Therefore, Descartes goes on, I need to look very carefully at the idea of God that I find lodged in my mind. I have to look at this idea of a supreme being. If the ultimate order of the universe is capricious or evil—that is to say, if God is not good—then neither knowledge nor well-being can be pursued by man. If the absolute God-Creator-Maintainer is not good or if His will does not reach down through the whole of reality, then man's life has no certain direction.

With Descartes, the ancient idea of the Source-Creator of everything that exists has become translated into the language of science. Sensitive to the way in which the Church had attached itself to the verbal formulas of Scholastic Christianity, Descartes was extremely cautious in his translation. Nevertheless, the revolution he helped to bring about lies precisely in his profound ability to restate an aspect of the ancient idea of levels of reality, levels of mind, levels of will and power in the universal order.

This achievement is what lies behind Descartes's proof of the existence of God. It is, of course, no proof at all in the conventional, logical sense of the term. Here, as elsewhere, Descartes's philosophy can be criticized for its flaws—and, in fact, no other great philosopher of the modern era has been castigated as much as Descartes. He has been called the chief culprit of the ecological crisis because he argued for a stringent separation of the realm of mind and the realm of matter, an argument which helped to generate the modern view of man as lord and master over nature. His strong distinction between the knower and that which is known has been denounced by existentialist philosophers as the chief cause of modern man's sense of alienation from the world he lives in. He has been widely scorned as the philosopher of radical dualism who persuaded a whole era that there is an unbridgeable division in the structure of reality and human nature, the division between consciousness and the material world.

But Descartes is no dualist in this sense. There is, he argues, an all-pervasive Power and Mind outside of time and space which yet penetrates all time and space, penetrates downward into the human mind and the material world simultaneously, and which gives all orders of reality their structure and function. This is an aspect of a very ancient idea lying at the root of every great spiritual teaching that the world has known. Descartes used a new language to express this idea, the language of science, the language of logic and reflection divorced from the language of Church dogma. Man is so familiar with this idea of God as the Source-Creator-Maintainer of the cosmos, that he has ceased to feel its extraordinary quality and tends to think of it as a general, common, ordinary concept that just floats around in people's minds nourished by superstition and naive religiosity.

Descartes, however, feels the greatness of this idea and restates it in the language of knowing, rather than in the language of believing. This language had been in existence centuries before Descartes—starting with ancient Greece (especially Aristotle) and gathering strength in the medieval era in the great Scholastic philosophers. But it was for Descartes to separate this language completely from religious dogma and give it new life of its own. Not long after Descartes, this language was to become what we know as modern science.

Feeling the greatness of this idea of the highest level of reality, mind, and will—this idea of God—Descartes steps beyond the bare truth of *I think, therefore I am*. He asks himself just the sort of question we need to ask about great ideas—of course, in his own way and with somewhat different emphasis than is appropriate for us. He asks: Where did this idea come from? How did the representation of absolute reality come into my mind? Because he senses the greatness and scale of this idea, he knows that he could not have invented it himself. He then posits his conclusion, which seems so strange to our strange minds: The idea of God proves the existence of God! Seeing, observing myself, I know that there is nothing in my ordinary mind that could have created an idea of such simple, bold, and ultimate truth. This idea of perfect Being that lights up my mind could not have been produced by this mind, which I observe to be fastened, limited, swayed, and torn by subjectivity, fragmentary sense perceptions, egoistic impulses. Then, where did it come from? It could only have come from God Himself! Great ideas prove the existence of great Mind and great Being—which the Christian religion names God the Father and Creator.

All this Descartes puts in logical form, as had been done centuries before him by the Scholastic philosophers. The idea of a perfect being implies its existence because, by definition, a perfect being that did not exist would obviously not be a perfect being. In its various forms, this argument is known as the *ontological proof* for the existence of God and was argued by St. Anselm, St. Thomas Aquinas, Moses Maimonides, and other philosophers of the medieval era. Logically, it is full of holes, tricks, frustrations. By the canons of strict logic and conventional rules of inference, it is utterly unconvincing.

But the logical form is only that—a form. Through this form of expression, which was then just beginning its ascension in the fashions of thought of the modern world, Descartes becomes the channel of an idea about levels of reality that has existed in all great teachings through time immemorial. Through Descartes and the other philosophers of the early modern era, this idea has reached down to us and, however weakened and automatized its expression, has retained its power to help human beings sense a greater scale of reality than the one that meets them in the problems and complications of everyday life.

God not only creates, He maintains—so Descartes tells us. The higher level of reality, the mind and force that pervades the whole, also reconciles and harmonizes the two disparate realms of mind and matter. "Out there" is pure matter, without consciousness or purpose—pure corporality obeying mathematical laws. "In here" is consciousness, selfhood, mind, "I." There is no relationship between them; they are two distinct metaphysical realities. Yet they are related in nature and in human life! Again, through God's power, a power that harmonizes opposites. Here, too, Descartes's "logic" becomes the channel of a very ancient great idea— the idea of a sacred force of reconciliation (called the Holy Spirit in some expressions of the Christian teaching).

Much more could be said here about Descartes, but it would distract us from our main purpose, which is to see how, even in the modern scientific era, philosophy has been the channel of awakening ideas, in this case the great idea of nature as a higher, all-inclusive reality containing levels of mind and will within which man must live and move and seek to discover the real purpose of his own existence. We are attempting to view modern philosophy in a way that is quite new. We are trying to follow great ideas downstream, trying to open passages that have become blocked in our contemporary world so that this ancient current can flow once again. Measured against the full expression of truth that we may presume is contained in the all-encompassing doctrines and teachings of an authentic path or way of self-transformation, the arguments of modern philosophers may well be criticized as fragmentary, imprecise, lopsided, and narrow. I have tried to apply such a standard in the earlier discussion of the teachings of Pythagoras. In that discussion I attempted to speak as one following ideas upstream—toward a vision of the great and integral source of awakening ideas where the seeker must ultimately confront Socrates; which means—through the intense and personal confrontation with a guide—to live through the shattering confrontation with oneself.

But our world, our lives are such that before we can hope to move upstream, we need to be helped to move downstream. Before we can struggle against the current of ideas flattening out into mere concepts, we must perceive the current itself and enter into it. Through this brief discussion of Descartes, we can see that modern man is moving away from the current itself, the ancient stream of awakening ideas. The God of nature has become the "integrity of the environment"—it is too far from the idea of nature; it carries no question; it is only a problem. A problem is something I must solve; a question is something I must experience. Through the experience of questioning, another faculty begins to stir and evolve in man, a faculty or power that is potentially higher than the mental and emotional functions which are in the grip of the ungoverned automatisms of fear and craving. This potential faculty within the psyche of man begins as the sense of wonder. As such, it is a child, powerless. Developed, it is Man. And only Man can solve the problems of "man." Therefore, we need to enter once again the stream of great ideas in order to magnetize the heart, the *eros*, the sense of wonder—but not to solve our problems. And yet, only in this way will our problems be solved. This is a staggering paradox that faces us as we are torn by the colossal problems visited upon us by our modern situation. Behind the problem, lies the Question. And behind the Question lies the answer. We cannot solve our problems without the development of a new power of mind within ourselves. Yet this power of mind begins with wonder, with *eros*, with our becoming "as little children."

The concept of the environment stands before us as a problem to be solved. Can we convert it into a question to be experienced?

CHAPTER 10

One Self: Two Worlds

I remember the precise moment when it occurred to me that my friend Elias Barkhordian was dying. I did not hear the word "leukemia" until months later when the final stages of the disease, which in those days was completely untreatable, had set in and he could no longer keep our regular rendezvous at the stone wall. I had known from the very beginning that he had some mysterious and serious illness. He would often have to cancel dates we made, or, when I telephoned, his mother would often say, in a peculiar tone of voice, he was "resting." Still, I half imagined she was simply pampering him—he was an only child.

One October afternoon—I remember it was the day before my twelfth birthday—we had just begun talking and I happened to be looking at Elias's ears, which had always fascinated me. He had no ear lobes. When I had once made a remark about that, he informed me that it was because he had been prematurely born. "The ear lobes are one of the last things to form in the human embryo," he said. This fact riveted me. I was dumbstruck by the thought that this living person, my friend Elias, was a sort of substance, like a clay figurine that could be added to in increments and that, had he stayed longer in his mother's womb, a little more substance would have been added to him. At the same time, he was *Elias*, the individual person. Was that also a substance that could be added to or taken away in gradual increments?

On that particular October day, looking at his ears and thinking about his illness, something like the following came to me: He was born too soon and he will die too soon. But what was *he*? Was *he* something that was dipped in a wrong way in the river of time? The river of existence? What did *he* have to do with time? Where did *he* come from? Where was *he* going? And what of *me*? What am *I*? I was once a baby; now I am twelve years old. Where did I come from? Where am I going?

I don't remember how we began that afternoon, but I remember staring at Elias as though if I looked hard enough I might see what he really was behind his face. I had the vague but very strong feeling that somehow Elias really knew what he was and that it was an odd kind of secret he was keeping from me. I felt that if I knew what kind of questions to ask him, he would tell me. The thought that he did not have long to live somehow increased my certainty about this.

Suddenly, I was struck by the realization that perhaps he didn't know after all. I looked at myself, and again asked myself: What am I? I don't know what I myself am, so why should Elias know what *he* is? For a moment, the whole thing struck me as ludicrous and depressing. I *am* . . . something, something or other, obviously. But I don't know what! And Elias, too, is something or other and he doesn't know what! If he dies it will be without ever having known what this something or other was! If I die, it will be the same story.

It was the same sort of feeling we both had shared a few weeks before when we were talking about the planet earth and how little science knew about the make-up of the earth's core. We both found it ludicrous and strange that science knew so much about the planets and the stars, which were so far away, but that no one knew what was under the surface of our own planet. I would fall asleep at night picturing all sorts of devices for boring down deep into the earth—but in my imaginings the earth always collapsed in upon them a mile or so down.

That afternoon I felt that if I could see into Elias's death, I would be able to see into what he was. I felt absolutely no sadness about him—that only came later.

I'm sure Elias realized that I was staring at him strangely, but it didn't seem to disturb him. As always, he remained unruffled behind his broad, serene forehead. I wondered, "What is behind that forehead?"

Neither of us had the language to speak about this sort of question. We started talking about the brain, but it was only when the subject of sleep and waking came up that I began to feel we were coming closer to the mystery.

"I wonder what happens to a person when he falls asleep?" I said. "Where does he go?"

For the first time in all our conversations, Elias did not have a ready answer to a question. This pleased me. Part of our game was the pleasure in stumping each other with difficult questions—but only part, and not the most important part by any means. Elias was rarely stumped for long—he always had some scientific information to throw in, no matter what the subject was. This time, however, he could find nothing to say. This made the moment incredibly serious. He turned his head away from me and looked down at his lap. He suddenly seemed to me very old.

The pressure of the silence soon got to me, however, and I went on to talk about the time I had been given sodium pentathol for a tooth extraction. I was counting backwards from one hundred and when I reached ninety-eight I saw myself disappear. How could that be? How could I disappear and still see—even if only for a split second—that I was disappearing?

Elias had also had some experiences like that and we spent the rest of the time swapping stories—"tales of consciousness," so to say. We talked about dreams and dreams within dreams. We toyed with the idea that perhaps we were dreaming then and there. "Suppose I'm in bed right now," said Elias, "dreaming that we're sitting here. Suppose the whole of our life is a dream."

We both liked that thought and then we started joking and, for some reason, we began vying with each other to see who could make the most vulgar and obscene noises. We soon surrendered ourselves up to helpless laughter. Elias laughed in a most peculiar way. Tears flowed copiously from his eyes—his laughter somehow never descended lower than his neck. His equivalent of a belly laugh could hardly be distinguished from someone showing the signs of shock and sorrow—his big face became contorted, as though in excruciating pain. In the midst of my own rollicking laughter, I had one fleeting impression of his laughter as weeping and the whole question returned again—what is *he* and what is going to die? I sensed the fact of my own death with tremendous clarity. Yet through it all, I went on laughing—*it* went on laughing—by sheer momentum. It was incredibly like the pentathol experience, this sensation of division in myself. As with the pentathol, the watcher had no language, no thought, only pure existence—fleeting, momentary, intensely alive and calm.

Many years later I acquired the language that corresponded to this sort of experience and this indestructible question about appearance and reality. In myself and in nature the reality behind the appearance exists in broad daylight, radiating ceaselessly. Yet something obstructs my attention to it. I consider myself to be my thought, my thinking—and my thought activity is not this reality, this pure being behind the appearances.

The idea of a real self behind the appearances forms the central doctrine of every great teaching and tradition throughout the ages. It is always intimately related to the idea of a higher or absolute reality behind the appearances in the whole of nature. In Buddhism the Buddha-nature, enlightened Mind, is the true reality of myself and the universe. In Hinduism, *Atman*, the real human Self, is *Brahman*, the Absolute God-Creator-Destroyer-Preserver. In Judaism the name of God is I AM, and Christianity reconstitutes this idea through the teaching about the Holy Spirit which is ultimate Self (the "personal God," the Father) acting and suffering within all men. This idea is expressed and developed in all teachings with extraordinary richness, subtlety, and complexity—especially where it is a question of psychospiritual practices guiding the struggle for ever-deepening human experience of this reality.

The overall idea, sometimes stated with heartrending simplicity, occurs everywhere, whether or not experience of it is in question.

Pythagoras spoke of a *central sun* of the whole cosmos that was also within each man. Plato writes of the highest Being as like the sun within and outside of man, where reality and the Good are one and are the ultimate active, causal power—the soul in man, the power of which is to harmonize all the functions and appearances within individual human nature. In short, the idea moves like a great river through the history of our culture, fed by currents that originate in many and various minds and teachings.

When modern science and the scientific approach to knowledge took root in our world, there seemed to be no place for this great and universal idea of the one Self behind the world of appearances. From the point of view of the scientific attitude, it was an unverifiable idea, something that could not be seen, a mere object of belief. With extraordinary integrity and honesty, those philosophers who first articulated the universal vision of modern science often excluded this idea from their formulations. For these great thinkers, the essential thing was to avoid fantasy and the mental tyranny of dogmatic belief and the self-deceptions wrought by authoritarian metaphysics. We who now see the limitations of these early philosophers of science—because we have been provided with knowledge about ancient teachings that they could not have had—would be foolish not to recognize the courage and love of truth which they exhibited in refusing to believe anything they could not verify for themselves. Contemporary man's passive, mechanical acceptance of sensory experience as the sole standard of truth must not be confused with the active, searching inquiry of these early empirical philosophers.

Like Descartes a century before him, the eighteenth-century Scottish philosopher David Hume sought to separate knowing from the passive, automatic acceptance of beliefs and speculations about reality. Hume relentlessly exposed the slavery of the human mind to psychological habits, and the influence of his analyses is still very strong, even though almost no one is able to maintain Hume's rigorous standards of skepticism and self-honesty.

"There are some philosophers," he wrote, "who imagine we are every moment intimately conscious of what we call our Self; that we feel its existence and its continuance in existence; and are certain . . . both of its perfect identity and simplicity."* But, says Hume, there is absolutely no evidence, no experience of this so-called Self—it is only a construct which the automatisms of the mind fabricate out of impressions and psychological events that have no necessary connection to each other, far less to a central, unitary self.

It is necessary, he continues, to observe oneself dispassionately, scientifically; it is necessary to be as empirical about oneself as the scientist is about external nature. When we do so, we see that there is no experience, no impression of any such thing as a persistent, enduring self. "For my part," he writes, "when I enter most intimately into what I call *myself*, I always stumble on some particular perception or other, of heat or cold, light or shade, love or hatred, pain or pleasure. I never can catch *myself* at any time without a perception, and never can observe anything but the perception. When my perceptions are removed for any time, as by sound sleep, so long am I insensible of *myself*, and may truly be said not to exist."**

For Hume, truth, true ideas reflect or mirror experiential facts, what he calls impressions. By this scientific standard, there is no true idea of self or person persisting through time—because there is no impression, no experience of such a thing. "If any impression gives rise to the idea of self, that impression must continue invariably the same through the whole course of our lives, since self is supposed to exist after that manner. But there is no impression constant and invariable. Pain and pleasure, grief and joy, passions

*David Hume, *A Treatise of Human Nature*, Part IV, Section VI.
**Ibid.

and sensations succeed each other, and never all exist at the same time. It cannot, therefore, be from any of these impressions, or from any other, that the idea of self is derived, and consequently there is no such idea."*

Therefore, Hume concludes, a man is "nothing but a bundle or collection of different perceptions, which succeed each other with an inconceivable rapidity and are in a perpetual flux and movement."** There is nothing in the human psyche which remains unalterably the same even for one moment. "The mind is a kind of theater, where several perceptions successively make their appearance, pass, re-pass, glide away, and mingle in an infinite variety of postures and situations."† However, the analogy of the theater must not mislead us, says Hume. There is no *place* where these perceptions and impressions come into being and pass away. These ephemeral impressions *are* the mind, they are not *in* the mind.

The effort of pure, unalloyed self-observation led the great Scottish philosopher to deny the most cherished and deeply embedded assumption of every human being: the belief in one's own existence as an individual self. On this score, it is very tempting to compare Hume's conclusions with those of Buddhism. Like Hume, Gautama Buddha taught that man's belief in the reality of the self is an affliction, a disease of thought and the principal cause of all human misery and ignorance. However, the similarity to Buddhism weakens when we remember that the teaching of the Buddha is based on the existence of another power of consciousness which illumines all these fleeting, fragmentary aspects of the "self" like a great sun. The Buddhist does not use the term "self" to refer to this fundamental reality of great consciousness, because the term conjures up wrong pictures in the mind. Nevertheless,

*Ibid.
**Ibid.
†Ibid.

the whole message of Buddhism is that behind the appearances of nature and of my inner nature, there is a supreme, absolute reality of mind, consciousness, a supreme I AM that is not simply a "self," or "ego." Were the Buddhist to speak to Hume, he might ask him: "Who or what is aware of all these impressions and perceptions?" But there was no one to ask this honest philosopher, Hume, that question.

Hume has in effect destroyed the illusion of the self, an illusion which it has also been the task of the great teachers of the past to destroy. Through this destruction of the illusion of self, man is brought to understand that he, himself, is a world of appearances just as the external world is a world of appearances. In this fashion, the great and indestructible idea of the reality behind the appearances is everywhere implied by every honest scientist of the self, including Descartes and Hume, who would no doubt have been surprised to be placed in the company of Gautama Buddha or the Vedic seers or Jalalladin Rumi, as well as Pythagoras and Socrates. Not that they or other of the early modern philosophers attained in their being what was attained by the masters of the path of transformation. However, ideas introduced into the stream of human civilization by these masters flow also through the towering intellects of the philosophers as well.

Who or what is aware of these inner appearances? It is in this form that the great idea of an inner self-reality announces itself to us as we read these pioneering scientific philosophers. But when this question becomes only a problem to be solved, as it has become in our contemporary world, the current of this ancient and great idea ceases to flow. Just as the idea of nature is veiled by the contemporary problem of the environment, so the idea of the inner self is veiled by contemporary problems of individual identity. "Social role," "ego-identity," "personal uniqueness," "originality," "self-definition"—so runs the list of labels and words surrounding the "problem of the self," as it manifests in present-day psychotherapeutic theory, in medical and legal disputes about the definition of death or the rights of the unborn. We have made our inner nature into an inner environment; the awakening question, Who am I?, has become the tension-riddled problem of self-improvement and self-definition.

In the philosophy of Immanuel Kant (1724–1804), the ancient idea of a great reality behind the appearances receives a startlingly new formulation precisely because of the uncompromising honesty and clarity of Hume's skepticism. Kant's awesome attempt to harmonize the teachings of Christianity and the teachings of modern science was also an intellectual earthquake whose aftershocks continue to this day. It was Hume's philosophy, as Kant himself admitted, that first awoke the great German thinker from his own "dogmatic slumber."

It was Hume's analysis of the concept of cause and effect that startled Kant the most—even more than Hume's theoretical destruction of the idea of the self. Causation, Hume wrote, means a necessary connection between events or between impressions. All we can observe, both outwardly and inwardly, is that in some cases A is followed by B—whether A and B are external events or internal impressions. We never *observe* causal power; we never *observe* a *force* by which one thing brings into being or necessitates the existence of another thing. We never *observe*, we never *see* necessary connection, no more than we can ever see the self. The idea of causation and the idea of the self are both merely the products of psychological habits within our own minds. There is nothing "out there" or "in here" that corresponds to them.

Kant could not deny the integrity of Hume's analyses, yet he could not accept their implications both as regards the status of scientific knowledge and the status of Biblical religion. Like most of the great thinkers of the early modern era, Kant felt that science, especially as it had been brought by Isaac Newton, was the highest form of knowledge that man could have about the external world. The laws of physics were rooted in something indelibly true—as true as the moral laws which God Himself revealed to the soul of every normal human being. And yet—there was this Hume, this fact, undeniable, that no honest man could claim to have experienced the law of causation in the same way one experiences the data of the senses.

What to do? How to think about this impossible dilemma? The laws of the universe are certain, they are not capricious, they are not temporary conveniences; there is an implacable order of nature. Yet there is no direct experience of this order. I know, with utter certainty, that every effect must have a cause, although I have never seen or experienced causal power! Is the mind of man doomed forever to speak of things it cannot be sure of when it seeks to ascertain the deepest truths about reality? This cannot be, said Kant. In fact, he hated nothing more than mere speculative philosophy, the metaphysics of fantasy and imaginary realities. These speculative metaphysicians had for too long dragged the noblest endeavor of the human mind, philosophy, down to the status of gaudy daydreaming.

The fundamental order of nature is not a mere theory which man can entertain or dismiss at will. And yet there is no direct experience of it. Newton was describing reality above and beyond any individual, subjective preference; yet the laws of nature cannot be seen, felt, heard, or touched. Newton was describing the operations of God, yet no one can see these operations!

Kant's answer to this dilemma could be likened, as he himself likened it, to the revolution brought about by Copernicus—only this Copernican revolution concerned not the movements of the planets and the stars, but the very relationship of the human mind to nature itself. Until now, Kant says, man has completely misunderstood this relationship. Until now, he has believed that true knowledge, true ideas, involve a sort of mental mirroring of the order of nature—the mind forming concepts that accurately reflect external reality. At the deepest level, Kant says, this cannot be true. On the contrary, the opposite is true: *The order of nature conforms to the structure of the mind!* And not my mind, or your mind, but the structure of mind, reason itself. Reason legislates to nature—it does not simply obey it! At the deepest level of natural order, it is reason that is the active principle and nature that is the passive principle. Just as Copernicus had shown that the motions of the heavens are determined by the motion of the earth, so Kant demonstrated that the laws of nature are *put into* nature by the mind, not merely discovered there as something existing independently of the mind.

"Hitherto it has been assumed that all our knowledge must conform to objects," writes Kant in his preface to the *Critique of Pure Reason*, the single most influential work of modern philosophy. But, Kant goes on, this assumption must be set aside as regards our knowledge of the fundamental order of nature. If knowledge must always conform to objects, we could never have absolute certainty about the basic laws of nature, such as the law of causation. We do have such certainty—a universe that does not obey such laws is simply inconceivable—even though we have no direct, sensory experience of these laws.

> We must therefore make trial whether we may not have more success in the tasks of metaphysics, if we suppose that objects must conform to our knowledge. This would agree better with what is desired, namely, that it should be possible to have knowledge of objects *a priori*, determining something in regard to them prior to their being given. We should then be proceeding precisely on the lines of Copernicus' primary hypothesis. Failing of satisfactory progress in explaining the movements of the heavenly bodies on the supposition that they all revolved around the spectator, he tried whether he might not have better success if he made the spectator to revolve and the stars to remain at rest.*

Immanuel Kant's Critique of Pure Reason, trans. Norman Kemp Smith (London: Macmillan and Co., Ltd., 1953), p. 22 (Bxvi).

Kant therefore answers the skepticism of Hume by arguing that by the time we have any experience whatever of the world, we—that is, the mind—have already formed the world according to certain fundamental laws governing the operation of reason. Without these laws by which reason operates, we would have no experience whatever, no perceptions whatever. Hume claimed we can have no scientific certainty about such fundamental things as causality in the external world. Kant replies that we have certainty about reason itself and, since reason shapes our experience of the world, we can have certainty about the way the world must appear to us. Causality is a principle of mental operation—therefore, the world must appear as causally determined. These laws by which mind operates are not merely psychological habits from which we can free ourselves. We are constitutionally unable to be pure skeptics about nature. No, these habits are actually laws of reason and understanding—and therefore, laws of perception as well. We are, as it were, condemned to certainty.

Hume and Kant are one in their hatred of dogmatic metaphysics and theology. As children of the age of science, they both take arms against what they consider the dreams and fantasies of speculative metaphysics, with its claims to special sources of knowing and "higher" experiences of God and nature. But Kant will not rest with the skepticism of Hume; he brings back certainty into human knowledge of the world. Only now, it is no longer certainty about the world as we ordinarily conceive it. No, in Kant the world itself is a product of the interaction of human reason and something "out there" which we can never know. We have certainty—but it is certainty only about the contribution of reason to experience.

It is in Kant's sense of the "out there" that the ancient current of great, awakening ideas runs strongest through his philosophy. Human knowledge is "condemned to certainty" about the object-world which it constitutes through the inescapable rules by which it synthesizes the raw material offered by the senses. We can know only appearances and we can know with certainty only what the mind inescapably contributes to the structure of these appearances. What of the world behind these appearances? Must there not be a reality "out there," a world of the thing-in-itself that exists independently of the human mind? Can we know it? Can man have knowledge of the world, of reality, as it is in itself, prior to or independent of its shaping by human understanding? Is knowledge of the real world "out there" possible for us?

Kant's answer to this question creates a tension and an energy of incomparable force in modern thought. His answer to the question, Can we know the world as it is in itself? is a towering, unmitigated *no*. We cannot know the world behind the appearances; we have no experience of the thing-in-itself. The mind is forever barred from that world. All our knowledge comes to us in the raw material of sense data shaped by the laws of operation by which the mind functions. Our minds have an idea of the reality behind the appearances, but it is only an idea, a concept—it has no "filling," no experience to support it; there are no sensory data to correspond to it. Causal law, time, space—all these are rules by which mind operates and shapes raw sensory data. The world as it is in itself—a world outside of time, where time exists no more; a world unlimited by space, a world of infinite greatness and fineness; a world unbound by causal determinism, a world of self-freedom and independent reality—such a world we can only imagine; we can know nothing about it; we cannot even know whether or not it exists.

Kant gives another name to this imagined world behind the appearances—he calls it the *noumenon*, from the Greek *nous*, the power of direct knowing. In giving that world such a name, Kant is expressing the idea of a power of the mind that could directly know reality in itself without the mediation of the senses. However, declares Kant, man has no such power to see directly into reality without the mediation of the senses.

It is impossible to convey here the overpowering brilliance and thoroughness by which Kant delivers this negative aspect of his philosophy in the *Critique of Pure Reason*. It is said that the playwright Heinrich von Kleist was driven to suicide by this notion that man is forever barred from knowing the world as it is in itself. In any case, modern thought has never been the same since. Modern philosophy has been stamped indelibly by Kant's refutation of the possibility of direct metaphysical knowledge of the thing-in-itself and, generally speaking, there are no longer metaphysicians to be found anywhere.

It is possible, of course, to refute Kant with one or two very simple remarks. The whole massive structure of the *Critique of Pure Reason* rests on assumptions that are, from a certain point of view, almost laughably weak—for example, Kant's insistence that there is no experience of noncaused events outside of space and time, and his dogmatic assumption that there is no such thing in all of human life as intellectual intuition. The reaches of human experience that have been vouchsafed in the mythic and psychophilosophical communications of the great masters of gnosis in India, Tibet, ancient Egypt, Pythagorean Greece, the Byzantine Fathers, the masters of the Kabbalah, and countless others show the limitations of Kant's vision. This, however, is "upstream" criticism—the sort that has been attempted in the earlier chapters of this work. It is inappropriate and presumptuous to attempt it here. We are not masters of the path; we do not have the experience these great traditions speak of—though it is not impossible for any individual to attain it. Furthermore, to compare Kant's thought with the thought of these great masters of truth is to compare teachings that lead upstream toward a life of self-transforming inner confrontation, with formulations and arguments that serve as "downstream" channels of great ideas into the general life of human civilization. Esoteric teachings are not philosophy. The former have meaning principally in the confrontation with "Socrates"; the latter call the heart of man to seek out "Socrates." Philosophy is for calling the heart within the mind; esotericism is for transforming the being. A great philosopher like Kant cannot guide the work of self-transformation; the scale of his thought and the precision of his formulations—among other things—are entirely inadequate to that task and it is wrong to measure his philosophy solely against such a standard. We need a downstream appreciation of philosophy quite as much as an upstream criticism. Great philosophy is a channel of truth moving downward to call man toward the search for himself. It stops at the portals of that search where Socrates stands and, behind him, Pythagoras.

To weigh or assess Kant's argument in the *Critique of Pure Reason* is therefore not of first importance. In general, criticism needs to follow, not lead, real feeling. Whether we are speaking about the education of young people, or the education of what is young and searching in ourselves, it is first of all necessary to support the love of wisdom, the sensitivity to universal ideas that throw the whole of our common life in question. To think in new categories; to envision life within a vast, new frame of reference; and, through that, to awaken and orient that impulse in human nature which is deeper and higher than ego—this is the first task of real philosophy.

And no one reading the *Critique of Pure Reason* to the end can fail to be touched by something tremendous in it, something that hints deeply and repeatedly at another scale of reality within which man lives and moves and has his being. Come to this book without being entirely driven by academic or professional motivations and you will see. Come to it after having yourself wrestled with the great questions of philosophy. Can God's existence be proved? Is there a first cause in the universe? Can reality be divided into the infinitely small? Does freedom exist anywhere in nature? If such questions have ever moved you to ponder what man is and in what world he exists, where he comes from and where he is going, you will find in the *Critique of Pure Reason* indications that the whole of our common human life and the whole of nature itself is penetrated by some unknown reality, access to which requires of man far more than the exercise of thought and ordinary reason, no matter how brilliant or ingenious it may be and, of course, far more than even the intensest emotion. Every idea you have, every speculation you have pursued, every experience you treasure, all this is not enough and can never be enough to place you in authentic relationship to the real world behind the appearances—to God.

Kant could have produced the *Critique of Pure Reason* with its uncompromisingly negative assessment of human knowing only because at the same time he believed in the existence of a hidden reality streaming through the whole of man's life and the natural order. Hume, apparently, did not have such a conviction or, if he did, it could not have been nearly as strong as that of Kant. Therefore, Hume backs away from an utter, entire skepticism about the powers of the human mind in its ordinary condition. No honest man can be a complete cynic. The fact that he is honest already gives the lie to cynicism. Hume's honesty is unsurpassed in the history of philosophy. Kant, unlike Hume, could find the energy to relegate the whole of human knowledge to the role merely of organizing the raw data of the senses—because he was certain that another "real reality" penetrated the whole world of appearances. The prodigious criticism of ordinary knowledge represented by the *Critique of Pure Reason* communicates the scale of this "real reality" as does no other work of modern philosophy. Kant's idea of the *noumenon* magnetizes the heart to the exact degree that his criticism of knowledge bursts the illusions of the mind.

Nowhere in the *Critique of Pure Reason* is the slightest shred of hope offered that man can know the reality behind the appearances—and yet this work could not have been written without that hope. It is in Kant's second great work, the *Critique of Practical Reason*, that he reveals the way to man's contact with the "real reality," and it lies in a direction that is, as it were, vertical to the whole argument of the first critique. To put the point simply: Inwardly, in his own heart, in his own will, man *is* a being, a real reality, and not only an appearance. *I am* both a psychophysical entity that obeys the laws of nature (which are at root given by the mind itself) *and* a thing-in-itself, an inhabitant of the noumenal world. My will, my resolve, my intention is utterly outside the laws of cause and effect, even though when my will expresses itself in action of any kind, that action enters into the phenomenal world. If I try to know myself through reasoning and scientific study, I am only one object in a world of objects. Insofar as I will, I am a being of the real world outside of time and space and ordinary causal law.

Kant's description of man's inner, noumenal being is breathtaking. This inner will, which is or can be my real self, is utterly unrelated to the self that I ordinarily take myself to be, and that others take myself to be. We need to look closely at how Kant characterizes this inner self of man. But we need to remember that in writing this about man, Kant has at his disposal only one kind of language for it—the language of what in the modern era has been called ethics, the language of morality. Through Kant's utter reconception of the idea of the moral law, his philosophy becomes the principal channel in modern times of the ancient idea of man's two natures—the two realities within man and within the universal order itself. This indestructible idea of the two streams within all of reality, two streams that do not meet each other except under the most extraordinary—divine, stainless, undefiled—conditions has never been presented with more force in any modern philosophy. Only Kierkegaard equals Kant in the power and clarity with which this idea is expressed in modern language.

Before quoting from Kant's formulations of this idea, it is necessary to call attention to the very thin line that separates the exalted idea of Kant from rigid puritanical moralism, the rejection of which has been one of the chief preoccupations of the contemporary era. In the language of morality, Kant is speaking about the metaphysical structure of man and the congruence of this structure with the whole of the universal order, including the absolute God, Creator, and Judge. Kant could not speak of levels of mind or consciousness, nor could he speak of ultimate universal energies manifesting themselves in the human microcosm as the impulse to perfect the inner being and serve the Highest. The language in which these ideas had traditionally been expressed had been irremediably degraded by the eighteenth century. Speaking then in the only language available to him, Kant presents the idea of man's two natures in the following way: The inner reality of human beings such as ourselves consists solely in the impulse to will the good—an intention that is inexplicable in scientific terms and that is utterly unrelated to the motivations and causalities of the ego or phenomenal self. All our appetites, inclinations, and motives are opposed to this incomprehensible intention toward the Higher. Kant calls this intention *the sense of duty*. This sense of duty, this inexplicable intention emanating out of the higher part of human nature, is the sole and only free movement within man, the only aspect of our nature not entangled in the natural laws of space and time to which everything else in the world and in ourselves is subject.

Man, writes Kant, cannot pretend to know himself as he really is in himself by means of the categories of understanding by which his mind automatically orders the data of the senses. Through scientific knowledge of any kind, man must always be an appearance to himself, not a noumenal reality.

At the same time beyond these characteristics of his own subject, made up of mere appearances, he must necessarily suppose something else as their basis, namely, his *I*, whatever its characteristics in itself may be. Thus in respect to mere perception and receptivity of sensations he must reckon himself as belonging to the *world of sense*; but in respect of whatever there may be of pure activity in him (that which reaches consciousness immediately and not through affecting the senses) he must reckon himself as belonging to the *intellectual (noumenal) world*, of which, however, he has no further knowledge. *

And now listen to how Kant, using the term *duty*, characterizes this inner, real reality of human nature as an intention, a *wishing* that is both completely separate from all the other functions of the mind and yet, by its very nature, is meant to command and rule over these functions, these thoughts, impulses, and inclinations of our ordinary self:

> *Duty!* Thou sublime and mighty name that dost embrace nothing charming or insinuating, but requirest submission, and yet seekest not to move the will by threatening aught that would arouse natural aversion or terror, but merely holdest forth a law which of itself finds entrance into the mind, and yet gains reluctant reverence (though not always obedience), a law before which all inclinations are dumb, even though they secretly counter-work it; what origin is there worthy of thee, and where is to be found the root of thy noble descent which proudly rejects all kindred with the inclinations; a root to be derived from which is the indispensable condition of the only worth which men can give themselves?
>
> It can be nothing less than a power which elevates man above himself (as a part of the world of sense), a power which connects him with an order of things that only the understanding can conceive, with a world which at the

---

Kant's Critique of Practical Reason and Other Works, trans. T. K. Abbott (London: Longmans Green and Co., 1873), p. 71. I have substituted the word "I" for "ego" in this passage, which was translated over a century ago. The German word is the personal pronoun, *Ich*. In the past century, the English word "ego" has taken on connotations diametrically opposed to the word as Kant uses it. The Latin word *ego*, of course, is also the personal pronoun "I." Nowadays, general parlance has "ego" associated with what Kant would call "the phenomenal self"—not to mention its general connotations of pride, and self-illusion.

same time commands the whole sensible world, and with it the empirically determinable existence of man in time, as well as the sum-total of all ends. . . . This power is nothing but *personality* [the I], that is freedom and independence of the mechanism of nature, yet, regarded also as a faculty of a being which is subject to special laws, namely, pure practical laws given by its own reason; so that the person as belonging to the sensible world is subject to his own personality [the I] as belonging to the intelligible [supersensible] world. . . .

This respect-inspiring idea of personality which sets before our eyes the sublimity of our nature (in its higher aspect), while at the same time it shows us the want of accord of our conduct with it, and thereby strikes down self-conceit, is even natural to the commonest reason. . . . It is the effect of a respect for something quite different from life, something in comparison with which life with all its enjoyment has no value. . . . The majesty of duty has nothing to do with enjoyment of life; it has its special law and its special tribunal, and though the two should never be so well shaken together to be given well mixed, like medicine, to the sick soul, yet they will soon separate of themselves; and if they do not, the former will not act; and although physical life might gain somewhat in force, the moral life would fade away irrevocably.*

Had Kant gone no further than to show, in the language and thought-forms of the scientific era, the profound twoness of human nature, his philosophy would still have to be ranked as one of the greatest expressions of eternal ideas in the modern era. Perhaps no other modern philosophical reflection of this truth

---

*Ibid., pp. 180–182. As with the term "ego," Kant uses the term "personality" to refer to the real self. I have therefore put the term *the I* in brackets for purposes of clarity.

about human nature (again, always excepting the writings of Kierkegaard) speaks so uncompromisingly of this fundamental division within the self. True, it is to be found in the teachings of Luther and in all the great visions of early Protestantism. But only in Kant is it expressed logically, systematically, coherently, scientifically— that is to say, in a manner corresponding to the emergent subjective qualities that have come to define the era we all live in. Man is both free and determined at the same time; in him there is both a self-initiative toward the Absolute and a mechanical totality of psychological functioning. The former is utterly incommensurate with the latter. Moreover, it is through this latter, through the mechanical totality of the mind, that the external world of nature is known by us. Scientific knowledge must inevitably present a godless world. But, like the self, the world also is twofold. Everywhere and in everything there is *two*: freedom and mechanism, two movements incommensurate with each other. In myself and in the whole of nature there is a reality and an appearance. The reality is freedom, mind, the realm of divinity; the appearance is mechanism, materiality, necessary connection without ultimate purpose. Incommensurate realms—that is to say, the realm of freedom and mind exists on a scale incommensurate with all the activities and efforts of my ordinary mind and self. It is logically impossible for me to penetrate into that world. No thoughts, concepts, or systems, however clever or profound, can bring me into that real reality. No mysticism, theosophy, metaphysics, or heroism of emotion and striving; no painful struggling and self-denial; no ex· ˌses of passion and sensualness can help me to storm my way into the realm of the Absolute.

One thing, and one thing only in myself points me toward the real reality: this inexplicable, illogical, and even unprofitable *intention* toward what Kant is compelled to call the moral law. But this one thing in myself has absolutely no relationship to any other power or impulse in my mind or body: *I am two.*

He who hears in this the ancient message of all the great

spiritual teachings of mankind hears rightly. If the Zen Buddhist stuns the Westerner by taking away all possibility of penetrating reality through the intellect, so also does the philosophy of Kant. If the masters of Hinduism, Sufism, or Hasidic Judaism speak of a great self and a lesser self, of a higher and a lower soul, and, in a certain sense, uncompromisingly set these two aspects of human nature against each other, then so also does the philosophy of Kant.

Of course, it cannot be repeated too often that Kant's philosophy echoes these great psychospiritual teachings only as thought, as ideas that magnetize the ego in the direction of the path of awakening and not as gnosis, guidance along the path itself. No philosophy, however great, can destroy the ego. Yet it is the role of real philosophy to bring the ego toward the threshold of the path that leads to the ego's own voluntary destruction as the ruling force in human nature.

Having established the absolute separation of two worlds or levels in man and in the universe, Kant now writes his third critique, which attempts nothing less than what had seemed impossible: the bridging of the worlds. It is not possible to bridge these worlds; yet this bridge must exist. It is not possible to forge a relationship between the movement of freedom toward God and the mechanisms of the mind; between the noumenal, inner self and the bio-social, phenomenal self that calls itself by my name; yet this relationship must be found!

What is there in myself besides knowledge and will?

What is there *out there* besides the world of appearances and the world of things in themselves? What could be the *third thing*, the third force that could bind together the free will and the mechanical mind in a harmonious relationship? I *am*—the real, noumenal self that moves toward God's absolute law; and I *am*—the ego, the self-object in a world of objects. Am I also *something else* in between these two movements that are in themselves irreconcilable, that do not know or influence each other?

Kant dreaded any cheap synthesis within the self of these two forces. His attacks against the mystics, theosophical fantasists, metaphysicians, and spiritualists are merciless, as are his trenchant criticisms of all pretensions to knowledge that fall short of the honesty of authentic natural science. In fact, had Kant disappeared before writing his third critique, were we to judge his philosophy only from his first two major works, his legacy would have been a great No to any possibility of bringing together within oneself these two realities. Even today, many people study Kant without attending to his third critique and come away with the impression that Kant split man into two incommensurate parts and left it at that.

More than anything else, this biographical fact about Kant—that only late in his life did he see the hope of a reconciling factor within man and the world he knows—communicates the immense scale of this *third thing* which he saw within human nature. Philosophers who came after Kant, such as Hegel, took up this third factor and began their philosophy with it. Hegel developed the idea of a third harmonizing force that binds opposites together into an awesome system of explanation.

Yet far-reaching and all-encompassing as Hegel's philosophy is, it communicates far less about the extraordinary nature of this intermediate principle in man than does the work of Kant. To have written the first critique—the towering and single most important book of modern philosophy—proving that man cannot know reality in itself and that all nature is mechanical; and then, years later, to have written the second critique—the most influential book about the freedom of the human will; and only then, with life going on and with great fame and renown resting upon these first two works, to have glimpsed the possibility of bringing together what had been proven impossible to bring together—this biographical fact about Kant transmits, more than does Hegel's entire system, what the ancient spiritual paths had always taught about this third thing in man: its subtlety, its elusiveness, its movement against all the laws of reason; its merciful harmonization as though from above into the heart of man, bringing together, like the holy spirit of Christianity, forces that are set against each other within the being of man—the peace, the reconciliation that surpasses all understanding.

Coming after Hegel, Kierkegaard saw this fact about the intermediate, too, and tore at Hegel for assimilating it into the structure of reason and the mind. But Kierkegaard wrote in a different philosophical language from Kant's and the latter is all the more remarkable for having expressed this idea in the language of science and logic. Kierkegaard brought back the ancient language of love, poetry, myth, and drama, which Kant could not and did not make use of.

Knowing all this about Kant, one picks up the third critique looking for this miraculous third thing that will harmonize the two forces in man and in man's relationship to nature. But here one finds a text that is far more obscure, difficult, and puzzling than the first two critiques. The third critique vibrates with the contradiction between vast, architectonic logical form and a content pulsing with the warmth of life. Here Kant seems to say there is purpose and consciousness behind the appearances of the natural world—but no, there he takes away the possibility of knowing such a thing! Here he gives us God—but no, there he says we can never know God! Here Kant seems to break away from the whole system meticulously constructed in the first two critiques—but no, there it comes back, stretched into new shapes to accommodate and fence in a vision of the universe that answers the hopes and needs of the human heart. In the third critique, the mind of Kant—that stupendously austere engine before which an entire era recoiled—takes on flesh, bone, and blood, entering into the round of living in a world that terrifies, delights, and humbles every mortal human being who looks out upon it in search of meaning.

What is the third thing? The third force that bridges worlds? That harmonizes the inner and the outer self? It is a certain unique *feeling*; it is *eros!*

The world as it presents itself to the ordinary faculty of knowing is a world of mechanically determined phenomena. The world as it presents itself to pure reason and the moral will is a world of things in themselves that can never be known. In what other aspect can we deal with the world? What other faculty is there in man? This latter question Kant now answers by saying that in addition to knowledge and the moral will there is in us a unique power of feeling, a function of the mind that brings impressions of pleasure and pain that are completely different from the pleasures and pains brought to us by the physical body or the emotions of the phenomenal self. It is not in our power to know the world as it is in itself, nor can we will into existence the moral order that we intend in our deepest self. *"But we can feel what we can neither know nor will."*[*] It is a feeling that is more like knowing than it is like what we ordinarily experience as emotion. It is a knowing that is more like emotion than it is like the ordinary effort of acquiring knowledge through disciplined empirical observation and theorization. It is spontaneous and free and yet, at the same time, it yields the impression of harmony both in ourselves and in the world outside us. It arises in us without strain or effort, yet it brings us toward and even into the experience of uncompromising universal order.

What name does Kant give to this feeling? It is the experience of *beauty*. Having said this, Kant immediately cuts away almost everything that people ordinarily mix in with what they call "beauty." Precisely understood, the experience of beauty contains nothing that is of any advantage or usefulness to the self, not even that which is socially, altruistically useful. Nothing that is even in its most refined form sensuously pleasant or desirable. In the experience of beauty, precisely understood, man experiences the autonomy and perfection of the noumenal world incarnated in the external world. The external object spontaneously assumes the form

---

[*] Edward Caird, *The Critical Philosophy of Immanuel Kant*, vol. II (Glasgow: James Maclehose and Sons, 1889), p. 416.

and order of intelligence and purpose, those very things that the mechanical mind can never know.

Again and again, Kant reminds us that our knowing mind cannot attribute this order to the world outside. And again and again he tells us that it is just this order that is felt in the experience of beauty—with a *certainty* that the isolated mechanical intellect can never reach or affirm. Does this produce another division within the self? Does the experience of beauty *war* against the knowledge offered by the mechanical mind? On the contrary, the experience of real beauty is precisely the result of the harmonious working of the two natures of man. In that moment the inner and the outer meet—and this is something that the ego, the mechanical mind, the phenomenal self can never understand. Nor does it need to understand it at *those moments*. In that experience, the intellectual mind is under the willing obedience to another force within the self. Beauty is the incarnation of the noumenal will.

There is more. The experience of beauty delights, lifts us, quiets us with a felt certainty of the harmonious contact between the two worlds outside and inside ourselves. Kant's philosophy, however, cannot stop at this. There is in us yet another aspect of this power of feeling where we encounter that which bursts all form asunder, but which yet draws us upward; an experience not of a moment of harmonious meeting of our two natures, but of something in external nature and in ourselves tinged with the awesome color of divinity, the ultimate I AM of reality itself.

The poet Rilke wrote:

> For Beauty is nothing but the beginning of a terror that
> we are still just able to endure . . .*

Comparing the experience of beauty with the experience of the sublime in nature, Kant writes:

*Stephen Mitchell, ed. and trans., *The Selected Poetry of Rainer Maria Rilke* (New York: Random House, Inc., 1982).

[The beautiful] directly brings with it a feeling of the furtherance of life, and thus is compatible with that which charms us and with the play of the power of imagining. But the feeling of the sublime is a pleasure that arises only indirectly; it is produced by the feeling of a momentary checking of the vital powers and a consequent stronger outflow of them. . . . Hence it is incompatible with that which charms us. And as the mind is not merely attracted by the object but is ever being alternately repelled, the satisfaction in the sublime does not so much involve a positive pleasure as admiration or respect, which rather deserves to be called negative pleasure.*

What is Kant speaking of here? It is actually quite simple: the confrontation between man and that which is immeasurably greater than him; but this force that is immeasurably greater *also exists somewhere within himself*:

Bold, overhanging, and as it were threatening rocks; clouds piled up in the sky, moving with lightning flashes and thunder peals; volcanoes in all their violence of destruction; hurricanes with their track of devastation; the boundless ocean in a state of tumult; the lofty waterfall of a mighty river, and such like—these exhibit our faculty of resistance as insignificantly small in comparison with their might. But the sight of them is the more attractive, the more fearful it is, provided only that we are in security; and we willingly call these objects sublime, because they raise the energies of the soul above their accustomed height and discover in us a faculty of resistance of a quite different kind, which gives us courage to measure ourselves against the apparent almightiness of nature.**

Critique of Judgment no. 23, adapted from the translation of J. H. Bernard (New York: Hafner, 1951).
**Ibid., no. 28.

The beautiful and the sublime are that which immeasurably exceeds the reach of the mind and the ordinary emotions, but which is yet *experienced* directly and undeniably—the one yielding an extraordinary joy and the other an extraordinary attraction upward and inward. The beautiful yields to man the impression that nature itself is art and that great art is the discovery of the real structure of nature—the world as suffused with purpose, intelligence, meaning; an intelligence that arranges the material of reality into a harmonious plan that can be sensed only insofar as the parts of man's own inner nature are also, for a moment, working together harmoniously. As for the experience of the sublime, the impression it yields goes beyond even this and calls man to search for that in himself which is the equal of God's own power. This call is sensed directly. In front of the sublime, I experience myself simultaneously as infinitely small and infinitely great.

This is *eros*.

This is the sense of wonder.

It is the seed of real moral and spiritual power, which can only begin with the actual contact within myself of the higher and lower, the inner and outer, the free will and the mechanical self. In front of the sublime, we are on the verge of occupying the place of Alcibiades in front of Socrates and in front of myself, my own two natures. In that moment, in that confrontation, what will I do? No philosophy can answer that question. But all philosophy leads us to it. "Thus," says Kant, "the virtuous man fears God without being afraid of Him."

In the words of one commentator:

> . . . the feeling of the Sublime is not only independent of sensuous interests: it is negatively directed against such interests, and, therefore, prepares the way for the higher moral interest. In this way it assists that process of abstrac-

tion (inner separation), which is necessary to make the moral law exert its full power over us. *

No wonder then that we can almost never *see* the other person behind his mask, or ourselves behind our own mask of personality. The inner, noumenal will is inaccessible to our ordinary powers of observation which operate only according to the categories of mechanistic logic or which are displaced by emotions of personal gain and loss. In exactly the same way, we almost never see the Self of external nature—call it God the Father. But it is possible for man to see, in the external world, the bridge between the freedom of God Absolute and the scientifically known world. This bridge is traditionally called the Creation, the relationship between spirit and matter. This bridge is another meaning of the great *personhood* of God—call it the Holy Spirit. For this to be seen, however, this bridge must exist in oneself, between one's own two natures.

This bridge is a new and higher power of feeling in man—the "peace," the relationship that surpasses the understanding.

Reality exists only when *I* exist. I can know *you* only when *you* exist. Then and only then do God, nature, myself, and my neighbor participate in the same scheme of being.

In this way, the feeling for truth brings one toward the entrance to the path of self-knowledge. Who will cross the threshold of this path?

---

*Caird, *The Critical Philosophy of Immanuel Kant*, p. 439.

CHAPTER 11

The Indestructible Question

The shock of Elias Barkhordian's death reached me in the following way. I was visiting him at his home where he had been confined for several weeks as his illness worsened. Instead of meeting him at the stone wall, I would stop by on the way home from school and usually stay there, depending on how he felt, until dinner time. Although he was getting thinner and thinner each day and was physically weak, his mind did not seem to be affected in the least.

In his house there was what was called a music room, a small, sunken porch enclosed on three sides by windows and with heavy, cream-colored velvet curtains tied back to let in the afternoon sun. In the room was a long, slender harpsichord and an ornate music stand with a straight chair placed in front of it. A cello stood in one corner with a silk shawl loosely draped over it. The room was at the back of the house, just off the elegant parlor, and looked out over a lovingly tended garden that now, in mid-April, was bursting with flowers—forsythia, iris, tulips, and wild roses. A chaise had been set up against the far wall so that Elias could lie back and read and look out at the garden. I would take the straight-backed chair from behind the music stand and place it next to the chaise. I remember that during our talks I had to squint against the sun streaming through the wall of windows.

On that particular day I did not go directly home after being with Elias, but instead joined a game of stickball that was being played down the street from where I lived. Suddenly, I noticed that it was getting dark and that I was already late for dinner. Exhilarated by the game and the intoxicating smell of spring in the air, I ran home at full speed and breathlessly exploded into our kitchen with my alibi at the ready. To my surprise, neither my mother nor my father showed any signs of consternation. Puzzled, I quietly put down my books, washed my hands at the kitchen sink, and sat down to the dinner table. Only then did my mother say, "I'm sorry about Elias."

I did not understand what she meant. They both knew about his condition—why should she suddenly say she was sorry? I went on eating my soup, warily moving my eyes back and forth from my father to my mother.

"You were late," she said, "so I just called Mrs. Barkhordian to see where you were."

My spoon dropped out of my hand and I jumped up as though a powerful current of electricity had just passed through me. Without saying a word, I raced out of the house, flying down the back stairs, my chest heaving with loud sobs. I ran back toward Elias's house.

I ran for what seemed an eternity. In fact, I did not seem to be running or moving at all. It seemed to me that I was standing still and the trees and houses were flying past me. When I saw the front of Elias's house, it seemed to be moving directly toward me. It seemed to have a face.

I came to a halt at the front gate. I could not just barge in. I began running again, this time to the end of the street and around into the back alley. Traces of daylight still remained in the sky and a red, swollen full moon had just risen at the horizon. I ran down the alley until I came to the back of Elias's house. I climbed the picket fence and stood still next to a rose bush. I was looking at the window of the music room where I had just been with Elias. The cream-colored curtains were drawn shut and a dim light filtered through them. They seemed like a huge, closed eyelid.

I stood and stared at that huge eyelid for a long time. Was Elias still there behind it?

During the weeks that I was seeing Elias at his house, the subject of death, his own death, came up several times. I was very unsettled by how calmly he seemed to regard it, almost as though he were looking forward to a new kind of experience.

It was about a week after his confinement had begun. I arrived as usual just after school. Mrs. Barkhordian, a woman with enormous dark eyes and jet-black hair, briskly ushered me to the back of the house and brought in a tray loaded down with a pot of tea, a plateful of homemade cookies, and a bowl filled with pieces of loukoum and foil-wrapped hard candies. She would stand there looking right at me and would not leave us until she saw me actually eat something from the tray.

This was a Monday and I told Elias about the show I had seen the day before at the Fels Planetarium: "The Origin of the Planets." I was surprised that he did not seem very interested—especially as this was a favorite subject of ours and we both were inordinately fond of the planetarium. But I went on talking. Elias seemed to grow restless. Finally, he interrupted me rather sharply.

"I've been reading up on leukemia," he said. And then he proceeded to relate everything he now knew about the process of the disease. My heart contracted as I listened to him explaining, with cool precision, how the production of normal red cells in the bone marrow is displaced by the production of lymphosarcoma cells. At first, I did not want to hear any of that. As Elias went on speaking about the physiology of the blood, I became more and more fascinated by the subject itself and was soon no longer even thinking about Elias! I was just sitting there gobbling candy and discussing the functions of the various types of blood cells.

Suddenly, I saw tears coming out of Elias's eyes. He fell silent and turned his head away from me, toward the garden. I also became silent. I thought that perhaps he was in pain and I started to get up to call his mother. Then he turned his head back toward me. Squinting into the sun, I saw that his whole face seemed to have gotten bigger and looser, as though it were melting. In a startling deep voice that came from far down in his chest, he shouted, angrily, "I'll never be able to *learn* about everything!"

His words, and the strangely powerful sound of his voice, went right through me. Fighting back my own tears, I heard myself saying, also in an abnormally deep voice, "I'll learn for both of us!"

Elias looked at me as though I were a fool. In the same loud voice, he said, "How do you know? Maybe you'll die soon, too!"

My whole body shivered. In that moment, my own death was again real for me. I no longer felt sorry for Elias. I, too, was going to die. An extraordinary vibration appeared inside me; I felt solid as a rock at the same time that the awareness of my own eventual death poured through me and terrified me. We remained looking at each other for what seemed a very long time. I did not feel higher or lower than Elias. We were equals. I broke the silence.

"Even if you weren't going to die," I said, "even if you lived to be a hundred years old, do you think you would ever solve the mystery of death?"

Elias turned his head toward the ceiling. Suddenly he seemed calm again. His voice became soft. "Maybe," he said.

What rose up in Elias Barkhordian and in myself during that confrontation with the fact of death? And why does it appear so rarely in the course of our everyday lives? Surely, the world seems what it is because man is what he is. The real world cannot show itself to the false self. That is what I take from this event. When the real self rises up, even if only as a seed, an embryo, only then do the outlines of the real world appear.

All authentic philosophy revolves around this truth about the relationship between the real world and the real self. The world is real only when I am real.

And when I am real, only then am I responsible; only then am I a moral agent. Because only then do my parts—even if only to a degree—obey me; or, as Kant would say, only then do I experience a contact between the higher and the lower functions in myself.

Philosophy, said Plato, begins in the experience of wonder. Very broadly speaking, the whole of Western philosophy is thereby characterized. Of Eastern philosophy, on the other hand, it has been said that it begins in the experience of suffering, in the encounter with death and human finitude. As it is written in the Vedas of India:

> In suffering all men Remember,
> In happiness no one who can.
> If in happiness man could Remember
> What need for suffering then?*

The legend of the life of Gautama Buddha tells us the same thing. Shielded throughout his life from the fact of old age, suffering, and death, the Prince Gautama, at the age of twenty-nine, sees for the first time an old man, a sick man, a dying man. So deeply do these perceptions reach into him that he abandons his family and his throne to seek out the causes of human suffering and the means of escaping it.

Thus it is said that Western philosophy is impelled by the search for knowledge, while Eastern philosophy seeks release from suffering.

---

*Philippe Lavastine, "Two Vedantas: The Best and the Worst of India," in *Sacred Tradition and Present Need*, eds. Jacob Needleman and Dennis Lewis (New York: The Viking Press, 1974), p. 135.

As literal characterizations of the distinction between the East and the West, this observation is of little value. The West contains quite as much as the East of the confrontation with human suffering; and the East contains quite as much as the West of the experience of wonder in front of the greatness of nature.

But as statements of the two fundamental sources of the search for meaning in life, this distinction has much to teach. Both confrontations—the awareness of that which is immeasurably greater than man, and the awareness of the contradictions and falsehood in which the life of man is enmeshed—can ignite *eros*. It might even be said that both confrontations are necessary, at least in some proportion. To sense the higher without at the same time seeing how far man is from living in relationship to it is to float into metaphysical, moral, or religious fantasy. Equally, to see the contradictions and negativities of life without at the same time sensing the existence of immeasurably higher possibilities for man is to fall into egoistic fantasies of self-pity, anxiety, or anthropocentrism in its various forms, such as scientism, existentialism, and secular humanism.

Behind the appearances lies the indestructible question of myself. In front of the sublime or, equally, in front of the fact of death, man is utterly in question—between two worlds, two movements in himself and in the universal order. In that state, for a brief duration of time, he is thrown out of the closed circuit of egoistic thought and emotion. Something rises up, shows itself in him, which we are calling *eros*, the sense of wonder, the love of being—it has many names. Equally, it is without a name—it is nothingness, emptiness, silence. Measured against this emptiness, everything else in life and in myself is mere appearance.

Eros has a quality of intelligence and feeling that can evolve toward the formation in man of higher powers of mind. The questions which man puts to himself as a philosopher can be answered only by this higher mind. Philosophy cannot answer the questions it asks. It can only—yet this is a great role—lead man to see and sense the need for the transformation of his inner nature. Philosophy shows us the limits of our world and our selves; it points, sometimes mutely, sometimes articulately, to another level of world and self.

The great philosophers of the twentieth century show us how philosophy can continue to play this role for contemporary man suffering, above all, from the problem of the impact of technology on the conduct of his life. In the writings of Ludwig Wittgenstein, for example, the problem of technology is transmuted into the great question that Western man began to hear from the very first moment modern science assumed its dominant role in our culture:

1. What I see, what I know, is a universe of death.
2. What I feel is life.
3. Which is real—death or life?

1. The world is a vast blind machine, an assemblage of inert facts. I am only another fact in that world.
2. But I who know this encompass the world that I know with meaning and purpose.
3. Which is real: What I know or that which knows?

1. I do not see God in the world or in myself.
2. Yet the world and myself exist.
3. Which is real: the facts *about* Being or the mysterious fact *of* Being?

These, and many other such formulations, circumscribe the central question that modern man faces in the overwhelming light and darkness of modern science. Facing only (1) and (2), the world and our lives in the world appear as problems to be solved; impossible problems inducing fear, confusion, hasty commitments to dream-values or nightmare-facts, tense assertions of individual power. But a prolonged confrontation with (3), the third term, produces—or rather, reveals—the seed of a new and higher power in the mind. The effort, born out of need and therefore in its way effortless, to stand in front of the third line, is the beginning of the free mind, the transition to the search for transformation. This search is a discipline, a work, and it requires precise guidance and help; it needs Socrates—in person. Philosophy's task is to bring man to Socrates. Without authentic philosophy, man touches the third line—the state of questioning in front of the two worlds—and instantly recoils backward toward a choice between (1) and (2). He seeks a solution to the dilemma of life and death, God and matter, freedom and necessity. There is no such solution.

That is to say, there is no such solution in the state of consciousness in which we normally exist. But to go beyond this state requires the development in ourselves of a power to attend to both halves of being, both movements, the whole of ourselves.

Insofar as the intellect shows us a world of illusion and appearance, it is necessary to contact the feeling for God and truth—without denying the intellect, but without being swallowed by it either. Such is the challenge facing twentieth-century man.

All around us we see the intellect, represented by modern science, dealing us solutions to the enigmas of our existence, enigmas which it identifies as problems to be solved. These solutions immediately break down into yet more problems. And this process goes on indefinitely. A problem is solved in a way that breeds new problems with new solutions, and each of these solutions breeds yet more problems.

What is the origin and nature of human life? New technologies and biological discoveries bring that question as a problem to be solved. When does death occur if we can prolong the biological functions indefinitely? What is the cause of war and hatred—when its result can obviously be the destruction of all life as we know it on our planet? The intellectual function represented by the new technologies has bred these problems—*but they first appeared among us in the form of solutions.*

The list continues: What is the mind if it can be replicated in the design of a computer? What is the basis of moral obligation when the biological consequences of sex are obscured and the biosocial function of the family is transmuted? What is truth and commitment when the sources of political, religious, and familial authority are no longer rooted in survival needs? What is happiness when pleasure is so available and so empty? What are our duties to our neighbor when our neighbor is a whole culture whom we know only through the channels of journalism, warfare, and huge impersonal forces of economic competition and fear? What is knowledge of the world we live in if this knowledge comes to us mainly through newspapers and television and easy-to-read books?

In sum, the life of modern man—seen as though from outer space or from another dimension of time—appears as a huge being in whom the intellectual function has taken over the governance of life, and, as it must, has failed to bring order and simplicity into life. On the contrary, by thrusting its solutions upon the instinctual, physical, and feeling functions of the human organism, it has brought more complications and unhappiness into the life of man. The solution of specific external problems has been balanced by the eruption of unprecedented confusion and anxiety in the inner life. The intellect, by itself, is not mind—mind is made up of far more that exists within the human structure, and only mind can answer true questions, only mind can rule man. We are immoral because we do not have mind; we have only the isolated intellect, which is the hired employee, the imitation of mind.

Mind, real consciousness, is born in the confrontation between great reality and our present false condition; the confrontation of being and appearance, truth and inauthenticity. *Mind is born as and from* eros. And *eros* is born out of the union of gods and mortals—the encounter between real ideas and the human ego. In front of real ideas, I become still. I am in question; I am shocked by what I am and I feel the measure of what I am meant to be. In that state, I can sense the reaching down of my weak attention toward the real springs of human action, the organic life within me. It is said that only God knows man in his entirety. For us that means that in front of "God," in front of universal truth, a force of knowing is activated in me that can penetrate into the real springs of human action. Wonder, the love of truth, is the real seed of moral action. But not the truth as it is defined by the imitation mind that we call by the grand name of *reason*.

The great philosophers of the twentieth century can continue to serve as channels for ancient ideas whose function in the turn-over of life has always been to bring man to the state of self-questioning and the search for Socrates. The two most influential philosophers of this century, Ludwig Wittgenstein and Martin Heidegger, have each in his own fashion injected into our contemporary culture the idea of the two worlds—along with the indication that the world behind the appearances cannot be seen by the ego. Each tells us that we are confused, fragmented, inauthentic beings separated from reality by an impenetrable wall. Each tells us that we cannot live without moving mysteriously, inexplicably, to and fro through that wall. Each speaks of our two natures, ego and real self-being, as two aspects of the whole which can only be bridged through an inner event of such newness and upheaval that we have no words for it. Having no words for it, we must seek this bridge in silence or we must create a new language that can guide us toward the search for the whole of our being. Wittgenstein represents the former alternative; Heidegger the latter.

Both philosophers bring us in front of the inauthenticity of ourselves as we are and both point to another realm, another level of life that calls to us. Wittgenstein takes away our illusions about ourselves and leaves us with a *void* in which the new life, the new inwardness is to be sought. Heidegger creates a new *fullness* of concepts in which our illusions about ourselves are presented as aspects of life which we must see and accept without being fooled by them. In the realm of thought, the realm of philosophical speculation, Wittgenstein is like a Zen master thrusting before us the incapacities and unrealities of the ego; Heidegger is like a spiritual metaphysician surrounding our desiccated and impotent intellect with a powerful new orientation toward life and the cosmos. Both bring us forcefully to the question "Who am I?" And to both of these philosophers, twentieth-century science has no answer and no escape. They include science; they do not fight it or ignore it. We will look closely at one of these philosophers and try to hear the ancient truths that sound anew in his work.

Ludwig Wittgenstein was born in Vienna in 1889. As capital of the mighty Austro-Hungarian Empire, an empire that was to crumble without leaving a trace in the earthquake of World War I, Vienna in the early decades of this century was the epitome of the European civilization of our era. Not only were many of the seeds of what we now call "modernity" sown there, but the rebellion against modernity—a rebellion that characterizes our contemporary culture as well—found one of its first and fullest expressions there.

In this Vienna,* the composer Arnold Schoenberg was inventing a new logic of music, designed to purify this art of all inauthenticity, all secondhand emotions, in order to penetrate the realm of pure musical ideas. Abandoning the tempered scale in favor of the newly constructed twelve-tone scale, Schoenberg sought to create a music that could touch a deep, essential capacity within the human mind behind the appearances, behind the culturally conditioned responses of like and dislike. For Schoenberg, the beautiful in music was only a by-product of the composer's search for truth, and his compositions, which sound so cold and dissonant to many people today, were an effort to break through the

---

*Allan Janik and Stephen Toulmin, *Wittgenstein's Vienna* (New York: Simon and Schuster, 1973).

egoistic emotions into a reality accessible only to the feeling for truth. That Schoenberg perhaps failed in this effort—that his music was perhaps only a subjective intellectual effort cut off from the real world of subtle feeling—should not blind us to the fact that his aim, as stated, corresponded exactly to the aim and function of sacred music in the great spiritual traditions of mankind.

In this Vienna, Adolph Loos was attempting to do for architecture what Schoenberg was doing for music. One of the fathers of the "functionalist" school, Loos stripped away all ornamentation (he wrote an essay called "Ornament and Crime"), whose purpose, he held, was to induce in people a delight in unreality and falsehood. Function rather than ornament was the architectural equivalent of truth. In the creation of artistic truth, artistic *fact*, the world of eternal and spiritual reality could be sensed without being formulated explicitly. That world transcended forms, especially the forms of expression favored by society, but it shimmered silently in the authentic and pure forms of the true artist.

In this Vienna also, Sigmund Freud was exposing the pathological hypocrisy about sex that afflicted modern society like a cancer. His method of psychoanalysis sought to tear away every mask painted with the colors of religion, morality, art, or manners and reveal the human animal beneath that mask. On this basis alone, Freud taught, and aided by objective scientific reasoning, mankind could begin its long-delayed journey toward reality.

In sum, the extraordinary intellectual and artistic ferment of this powerful center of culture converged on the installation in the life of modern man of *the idea of the fact*. Here logical positivism was also born, that school of philosophy which sought to rule out of human discourse any notion or concept that could not be verified by strict scientific observation. Vienna, in a sense, invented *the fact*, as it has come to be understood in the principal intellectual endeavors of the twentieth century.

What is this uniquely twentieth-century concept of the fact? Central to it is the belief that the world and the things in the world are completely neutral with respect to meaning and value. The human mind may impose such meanings and values on the external world out there but, in themselves, the world and the things of the world simply exist without any purposes or qualities of good, evil, beauty, consciousness, or meaning.

In itself, this view is not new—it has many precedents in the history of human thought. But in addition, the twentieth century has added the belief that the truths about this neutral world can be ascertained by refined sense perception aided by logical inference.

This addition also is not entirely without precedent, especially since the onset of the scientific revolution. What makes the idea of fact peculiar to the twentieth century is the further belief that simply by knowing the facts about the world a man will be able to orient himself with respect to the conduct of his life. That is to say, the facts have enormous value, but values are not facts. There is nothing good, evil, beautiful, or ugly "out there," but it is good and beautiful to know what is out there.

Behind this view is the assumption that man can observe reality free of the influence of his emotions and conditioning. This observation yields *facts*. Moreover, man ought to do this. Such knowledge is obligatory for everyone and, of course, possible for everyone. There is no court beyond the court of fact. And all men are summoned to that court. The clearest representation of this myth of the fact is what we now know as *journalism*. The journalist goes out and "gets the facts." He seeks to report only what he has observed and frames his hypotheses only on the basis of facts. If he goes in with a prior point of view, he either sheds such prejudices or makes them known both to himself and to his readers. His main service is to report *what actually happened*. It is assumed that he can see what actually happened, or at least that he can accurately hear what is said to him and can be aware if his knowledge is tentative and partial. Aware of these temporary limitations on his information, he can take steps to observe more or improve his methods of observation. But in all cases he is duty-bound to stick to the facts. One fact is worth a thousand interpretations.

Understood in this way, the whole of modern science is best seen as a mode of journalism. Like the journalist, the modern scientist is duty-bound to discover the facts—those inert single truths about the neutral material world out there. His hypotheses must be based on these facts. He is obliged to open his eyes, refine his techniques of perception, and then to exert his intelligence in organizing the facts into a useful theory. The scientist is no more and no less than a *journalist of nature*.

In their brilliant study of the early cultural milieu of Ludwig Wittgenstein, Allan Janik and Stephen Toulmin single out one central figure as the dominant intellectual influence in Habsburg Vienna before World War I—the journalist Karl Kraus. As editor of *Die Fackel*, which he termed an "antipaper," Kraus sought to expose the layers upon layers of corruption and hypocrisy that he saw in the society around him. The most frequent object of Kraus's attack was the *feuilleton*, a journalistic form common in the newspapers of the time in which subjective opinion, wit, and *bon ton* literary style slanted the reporting of events beyond all hope of ascertaining objective truths. The *feuilleton* was for Kraus a symbol of the widespread corruption of morals and intellect rooted in the pervasive confusion between values and facts. His mission was to make people morally aware of this distinction in all aspects of life—art, science, politics, religion. The key to this mission was honesty and clarity of *language*.

The world of values is altogether distinct from the world of facts. What is this world of values, this sphere of universal reality which cannot and must not be spoken about in the same way one speaks of scientific fact—which perhaps must not be spoken about at all, but only *shown, demonstrated, incarnated* in art or life in the world? This world, this realm of values is not, surely, the realm of likes and dislikes, emotional reactions, preferences, egoistic attractions and repulsions; it is not the world of opinions and inclinations—no more than the ethical realm was for Immanuel Kant. It is a realm of immense scale—but what is it? How to locate it?

The work of Ludwig Wittgenstein, arguably the most influential philosopher of the twentieth century, represents a response to this question which, for sheer integrity and purity of execution, has few equals in the whole history of modern philosophy. Both in his early and later work, which on the surface seem bewilderingly different, Wittgenstein sought to separate the two worlds of man through attention to man's language—which for Wittgenstein is identical with his thought and, to a certain extent, with his comportment in the world. For Wittgenstein the two worlds may be called the world of language and the world of silence. In the light of all that we have said in this book, we may identify these two worlds of Wittgenstein as the world of intellect and the world of authentic feeling; the ego and the I, the phenomenal self and the real self, the outer and the inner—in short, we may read in Wittgenstein's philosophy a purely contemporary statement of the ancient idea of the two fundamental movements in reality and in ourselves. Like Plato and Kant and most of the great philosophers of the West, his writings serve to bring man in front of these two opposing realities in order to awaken and support in him the love of truth and being.

Before sketching Wittgenstein's own expression of this ancient idea, it is necessary to consider one other influence that was acting in the intellectual ferment of his Vienna and which clearly acted upon him throughout his whole life. Here, finally, we stand in front of the towering figure of Søren Kierkegaard.

It will no doubt come as a surprise, even a shock, to some students of modern thought to hear it suggested that the great nineteenth-century Dane exerted a decisive influence upon Wittgenstein. Kierkegaard's role in the development of existentialist philosophy is well known—that philosophy which, generally speaking, fought against the scientific view of man and man's place in the natural order and which argued for man's radical freedom and self-determination. How could Kierkegaardian ideas have influenced the philosophy of Wittgenstein, which has been taken by many to epitomize the analytic, scientific, hard-headed battle for fact as against metaphysics? Yet the truth seems to be that Wittgenstein understood Kierkegaard far better than most Kierkegaardians who have intellectualized the teachings of that great Christian writer. The truth seems to be that Wittgenstein, rather than most of the official existentialist philosophers, is the authentic descendant of the man who wrote that the essence of the human task is to seek a relationship in himself between his finite and infinite natures, and that neither intellect, nor emotion, nor ethical social action, nor aestheticism can forge that relationship.

For Kierkegaard, the highest truth of which man is capable is an *event* that takes place within the psyche when consciousness simultaneously confronts God and the ego. Salvation, eternal happiness—such are the names Kierkegaard gives to the possible results of this confrontation. It is a demand placed upon man by God, and made possible for man by the shattering event of Christ. Man must turn, man can turn to both the Creator and to himself—but all within the self, within what Kierkegaard called "subjectivity." This turning toward both the higher and the lower in oneself Kierkegaard called *faith*. He spoke of it as a leap and, thereby, spoke of this turning as the only true locus of freedom in human nature. The head, the intellect, cannot comprehend or make this turning. The intellect, the rational, reasonable part of the self is part of the finite nature of man, part of the ego. Nor can this turning be made from the emotions—sexual, aesthetic, ethical—that govern the life of finite man. Faith is an utterly new feeling within the subjectivity of human nature. In front of God everything that man is comes into question, becomes as nothing. The beginning of faith is heralded, therefore, by something that can only be called dread, a felt perception of the nothingness of oneself in front of the higher. Yet in and through this dread lies the only real source of human happiness and authentic being.

To take God, in this sense, out of Kierkegaard's writings is to destroy his message. Yet this is precisely what many existentialist philosophers have done. Freedom, inwardness, for Kierkegaard exists only as man faces both God and the limited self and wills to attend to both. His powerful descriptions of this freedom simply cannot be taken as a general phenomenology of freedom as used to characterize the choices and struggles within ordinary life. This is a freedom that exists only when the two worlds are confronted. To divide the everyday world, the world we ordinarily know and in which we suffer, into two halves which only seem like the two disparate realms, is to mimic Kierkegaard and corrupt his teachings. This is an example of mixing levels of reality, of confusing fact and value. The inner world is not the outer world. Conventional ethical, aesthetic, social, and intellectual choices and concerns are in no way understandable as manifesting these two altogether disparate movements of reality. One cannot derive authentic morality, the morality rooted in the demands of God, from that which the intellect can know and prove, or that which feelings of like and dislike, or impulses or mass social concern provoke in our lives. Human life cannot be guided by the *feuilleton*.

I take the writings of Ludwig Wittgenstein to be a stunning restatement of the Kierkegaardian perspective—and in the Kierkegaardian mode of an unwavering refusal to allow the form of what one says to contradict the content. But where Kierkegaard speaks of human existence, Wittgenstein speaks of human language. Taken as a whole, Wittgenstein's writings show contemporary, scientific man both the logical structure of the ideal world his scientific language builds for him, and the fragmented, disconnected life his ordinary language actually lives for him. He mercilessly destroys the illusion that the fundamental questions of meaning and purpose can be solved by the ordinary intellect, by demonstrating that all the so-called problems of philosophy are rooted in confusions of language—that is, mixing levels of reality. Behind it all, unspoken except in the form of hints, there looms the being of another world both within and outside of human nature, a world unapproachable by language—that is, by the ordinary mind. Take care, Wittgenstein teaches, to keep these worlds separate.

Wittgenstein's first major work, *Tractatus Logico-Philosophicus*, was completed in 1918 when he was 29. It is a book of tremendous passion composed in equal measure of extraordinary intellectual rigor and mystical emotion. In no twentieth-century work of philosophy is the separation between the inner world and the outer world drawn with more zeal and purity. It is a work of youthful idealism in what is perhaps the very best sense of that often-cheapened phrase—a work of *eros*. In it, Wittgenstein seeks to dissolve the *problems* of philosophy while, at the same time, evoking in the reader a sense of wonder in front of the *questions* of philosophy. In a brief prefatory note, he writes:

> If this work has a value it consists in two things. First that in it thoughts are expressed, and this value will be the greater the better the thoughts are expressed. The more the nail has been hit on the head.—Here I am conscious that I have fallen far short of the possible. Simply because my powers are insufficient to cope with the task.—May others come and do it better.
>
> On the other hand the *truth* of the thoughts communicated here seems to me unassailable and definitive. I am, therefore, of the opinion that the problems have in essentials been finally solved. And if I am not mistaken in this, then the value of this work secondly consists in the fact that it shows how little has been done when these problems have been solved.*

Like Spinoza's *Ethics*, Wittgenstein's *Tractatus* is written in the form of a long mathematical argument. Where Spinoza used

---

*Ludwig Wittgenstein, *Tractatus Logico-Philosophicus*, (London: Routledge and Kegan Paul Ltd., 1955), p. 29.

the outer form of geometric proof to express the idea of God and higher states of human consciousness, so the *Tractatus* bodies forth the idea of the noumenal world by means of a sequence of apparently scientific-logical propositions about the instrument by which man knows the phenomenal world. What is this instrument? It is language, considered as thought. The essence of language is thought. And thought is the same thing as logic. But logic is a set of rules, a structure that is wholly transparent to itself— constituted by itself. Through logic, the mind organizes itself and the data brought to it by scientific observation. Through making clear to ourselves the logical structure of language, we can see the logical structure of our world and free ourselves from the unnecessary suffering bred by confusions to which we apply the exalted name of "fundamental philosophical problems." The intellect— logic and its manifestation in language—has nothing whatever to do with happiness, the perfection of the self, the experience of the meaning of life, or man's relationship to absolute reality—God.

The *Tractatus* begins with the following statements:

1.   The world is everything that is the case.
1.1 The world is the totality of facts, not of things.

And it ends with the most famous single statement of twentieth-century philosophy:

7. Whereof one cannot speak, thereof one must be silent.

Between this beginning and this end, Wittgenstein shows that logic structures the world we live in and that logic is the structure of the intellect itself. Science brings us observations which must take the form of facts, and all facts obey logical rules simply because anything that is known is by definition structured by logic. Logic tells us nothing about the world. It is only the rules by which we can know the world—that is, the rules by which we must organize the observations brought to us by the senses. Our knowledge exists in the form of propositions, statements which have an inevitable logical form and which function as a sort of picture or model of the world.

Over a century before Wittgenstein, Kant had argued that all material objects must appear in space and that space itself was not another object. Space, for Kant, was the general form in which all objects, if they are to be objects at all, must appear. Similarly, but with a much broader sweep, Wittgenstein shows that human life proceeds within *logical space*, and that there is no *meaning* to anything that purports to fall outside this "space." Most of the so-called problems of philosophy are merely disguised efforts to escape logic by means of logic—the intellectual equivalent of ghosts, nonmaterial objects that occupy space. Thus, early on in the course of the *Tractatus*, Wittgenstein writes:

4.003 Most propositions and questions, that have been written about philosophical matters, are not false, but senseless. We cannot, therefore, answer questions of this kind at all, but only state their senselessness. Most questions and propositions of the philosophers result from the fact that we do not understand the logic of our language. . . .
And so it is not to be wondered at that the deepest problems are really *no* problems.

But as the *Tractatus* proceeds to lay out the essential structure of language and meaning, hints about the other world behind the appearances begin to appear in the text. "Everything that can be thought at all," writes Wittgenstein, "can be thought clearly. Everything that can be said can be said clearly." Next to this statement, Wittgenstein writes that the aim of authentic philosophy is to "mean the unspeakable by clearly displaying the speakable."

In showing the logical structure of all meaning, Wittgenstein develops the method of truth-functional analysis in which all meaningful language can be broken down into atomic constituents that are either true or false. This technique was later to become one of the basic instruments by which the technology of the modern computer was developed. Thus a contemporary expression of the message of the *Tractatus* might be: Everything that we call thinking can be done by a machine! And the hidden messsage of the *Tractatus* would be: In order to experience the world behind appearances we must learn to see with another mind! Think with another mind! The computer cannot become free of its own structure. But we can free ourselves from the computer that is our everyday intellect.

As we approach the end of the *Tractatus*, the hints about this other world behind the appearances, this other power of seeing behind the internal computer, come more and more rapidly. Behind the appearances lies the Question—a *silence* which logic cannot enter, but which surrounds our lives. To be fully man is to be open, mysteriously, to the silence of being:

6.41 The sense of the world must lie outside the world. In the world everything is as it is and happens as it does happen. *In* it there is no value—and if there were, it would be of no value.

If there is a value which is of value, it must lie outside all happening and being-so. For all happening and being-so is accidental.

What makes it non-accidental cannot lie *in* the world, for otherwise this would again be accidental.

It must lie outside the world.

6.423 Of the will as the subject of the ethical we cannot speak.

6.431 As in death, too, the world does not change, but ceases.

6.4311 Death is not an event of life. Death is not lived through.

If by eternity is understood not endless temporal duration but timelessness, then he lives eternally who lives in the present.

6.4312 The temporal immortality of the human soul, that is to say, its eternal survival after death, is not only in no way guaranteed, but this assumption in the first place will not do for us what we always tried to make it do. Is a riddle solved by the fact that I survive for ever? Is this eternal life not as enigmatic as the present one? The solution of the riddle of life in space and time lies *outside* space and time.

6.44 Not *how* the world is, is the mystical, but *that* it is.

6.45 The contemplation of the world sub specie aeterni is its contemplation as a limited whole.

The feeling of the world as a limited whole is the mystical feeling.

6.521 The solution of the problem of life is seen in the vanishing of this problem.

6.522 There is indeed the inexpressible. This *shows* itself; it is the mystical.

6.53 The right method of philosophy would be this. To say nothing except what can be said, *i.e.* the propositions of natural science, *i.e.* something that has nothing to do with philosophy: and then always, when someone else wished to say something metaphysical, to demonstrate to him that he had given no meaning to certain signs in his propositions. This method would be unsatisfying to the other—he would not have the feeling that we were teaching him philosophy—but it would be the only strictly correct method.

7. Whereof one cannot speak, thereof one must be silent.

The *Tractatus* thus communicates more than any other single work of twentieth-century philosophy the immense scale of what it means to seek freedom from the tyranny of the intellect in man's search for the meaning of his life. Reality is twofold. Man is twofold. The computer mind functions to orient man in the world of appearances; the logic of language serves, or rather is, the activity of one part of human nature and orients us within, as it were, one part of reality. The other world, the reality behind the appearances, is not sayable, not knowable through the computer mind.

This, of course, is an ancient teaching—now channeled into the twentieth century. Confronting that which is unsayable, unknowable by the computer mind, there stands the feeling of the mystical—*eros*. This feeling—from where in myself does it come? There is in man an unsayable reality, just as there is behind the appearances of the universe. *That* the world is, is the mystical. But also: That *I am* is the mystical. Thus, the young Wittgenstein writes:

There are two godheads; the world and my independent I. *

This teaching about the two worlds was given out by Plato and channeled by Descartes, Kant, and others of the great philosophers throughout the ages. By the twentieth century, the expressions of these philosophers of the past had long since been captured by the ordinary mind. Ideas that pointed to another realm, another level of experience, had by Wittgenstein's time—our own era, that is—been overlaid with the forms of thought and expression used by the ordinary ego. They had therefore ceased to function in a way that touched *eros*. In this sense, great philosophers do not refute earlier philosophers, they revitalize the essential message that is

*Ludwig Wittgenstein, *Notebooks 1914–1916*, eds. G. H. von Wright and G. E. M. Anscombe (New York: Harper and Row, 1969), p. 74.

constantly being channeled into the world through authentic philosophy.

Wittgenstein wrote the *Tractatus* while he was serving in the Austrian army during World War I. During this same period, he writes to his friend, Paul Engelmann:

> About your changeable mood: it is like this: We are asleep. . . . *Our* life is like a dream. But in our better hours we wake up just enough to realize that we are dreaming. Most of the time, though, we are fast asleep. I cannot waken myself! I am trying hard, my dream body moves, but my real one *does not stir*. This, alas, is how it is!*

The philosophical writings of Wittgenstein's later years may be understood as an exposure of the nature of this "sleep," in which man is caught. Where the earlier philosophy, the *Tractatus*, bodies forth the need for a clean separation between the two worlds, the later philosophy, in addition to the many other things it accomplishes, may be understood as a revelation of the obstacles that stand in the way of awakening. Where the spiritual traditions of the past speak of the fallen human condition; of the state of illusion and ignorance; of life in the cave of shadows; of man's false sense of individual unity and personal power, Wittgenstein offers us a shattering picture of how our language actually operates.

Our language is our life—our state of consciousness, our behavior, our level of being. This ordinary language in which we live is a veritable tower of Babel, composed of heterogenous, fabricated "bricks" which we vainly imagine can be assembled together to reach upward toward unity, understanding, and absolute meaning. *Philosophical Investigations*, the great work of Wittgenstein's mature years, reads like a cinematic portrayal of the sleep of language.

*Paul Engelmann, *Letters from Ludwig Wittgenstein* (New York: Horizon Press, 1968), p. 7.

The language we live in, the language that lives us, the language that *is* ourselves, has not the structure and logic it ought to have. True, we can communicate pragmatically about certain material, physical activities—"This hammer is too heavy"; "That box is red"; "I want ten pounds of rice." But beyond this level, our language dissolves into a dream of hidden subjectivity and imaginary meanings. When we speak about ourselves or about anything beyond immediate, pragmatic activities, our language deceives us, takes us in without our knowing it. We imagine it is performing the same sort of function it performs when we speak about elementary, physical activities—because the grammar is the same. In fact, it does nothing of the kind. When we speak about God, or our inner life, or questions of an abstract nature, we are only living in a dream of meaning.

In the *Philosophical Investigations*, Wittgenstein has abandoned the mathematical-deductive form of the *Tractatus*. In his earlier work he was showing the precise logical structure of the mechanism of thinking—and the form of his writing mirrored that structure. In the *Investigations*, on the contrary, he is showing us that the life we live through our language corresponds not at all to that logical form—and the book itself reflects this. Instead of a condensed, mathematically ordered sequence of propositions, the *Investigations* is a loosely organized running commentary about the actual use of language in our ordinary life and the insoluble contradictions it conceals. The *Investigations* is an ongoing series of questions, like the quick, repeated thrusts of a sharp knife into a great, absurdly put-together beast. That beast is our illusory sense of ourselves. Wittgenstein runs alongside this huge beast, turning with it, stopping with it, badgering, stabbing, blinding it with his observations and questions. Will the beast stop, finally, and see itself as it really is? Will it—will we—wake up to the dreams of meaning that live our lives for us?

Let us look at one or two of these knife thrusts. Central to Wittgenstein's approach is his revolutionary concept of language-games. Our ordinary language—*as it in fact operates*—is nothing more or less than a loose cluster of language-games. There is no essence to our language. Our language—and therefore our life— has no single self, no internal unity of being, no *I am*. It is only a cluster of contexts and sets of rules, says Wittgenstein. And we need to stop imagining that it is higher or better than that!

Here we come up against the great question that lies behind all these considerations.—For someone might object against me: "You take the easy way out! You talk about all sorts of language-games, but have nowhere said what the essence of a language-game, and hence of language is. . . .

And this is true.—Instead of producing something common to all that we call language, I am saying that these phenomena have no one thing in common which makes us use the same word for all,—but that they are *related* to one another in many different ways. And it is because of this relationship, or these relationships, that we call them all "language". . . .*

By way of explanation, Wittgenstein continues:

Consider for example the proceedings that we call "games." I mean board-games, card-games, ball-games, Olympic games and so on. What is common to them all?— Don't say: "There *must* be something common, or they would not be called 'games' "—but *look and see* whether there is anything common at all.—For if you look at them you will not see something that is common to *all*, but similarities, relationships, and a whole series of them at that. To repeat: don't think, but look.**

*Ludwig Wittgenstein, *Philosophical Investigations*, trans. G. E. M. Anscombe (New York: The Macmillan Company, 1953), p. 31.
**Ibid.

Thus looking, Wittgenstein finds no *essences*, no single meanings in our most familiar words, and no single essence to our language itself. Just as Hume did not think, but looked into the self and found there no single I, no real self-identity, so Wittgenstein looks at our actual life of language and finds there at best what he calls "family resemblances," similarities among subgroups of word usages, but no permanent, single meaning that brings together any of the activities of our lives under a single, precise structure. Our language is a series of contexts into which we habitually smuggle the illusion of an overarching web of meaning.

Where does our investigation get its importance from, since it seems only to destroy everything interesting, that is, all that is great and important? (As it were all the buildings, leaving behind only bits of stone and rubble.) What we are destroying is nothing but houses of cards and we are clearing up the ground of language on which they stand.

What *we* do is to bring words back from their metaphysical to their everyday use.*

But where does our illusion of meaning, of order, come from? How has our language, our life, gotten into this fix—where we dream of fundamental realities, meanings, purposes, metaphysical essences behind the appearances? Wittgenstein commands us to stop, to stop and look, to stop dreaming we are what we are not— to "accept the everyday language-game" as it is and simply "to note *false* accounts of the matter *as* false."** How did it happen this way with our lives? Wittgenstein does not answer this question—and perhaps he would forbid us to ask it. Nevertheless, the answer is there in between the lines of this work of philosophical genius. The answer takes us back, back to the truth about the

*Ibid., p. 48.
**Ibid., p. 200.

human condition shown to Plato by Socrates, and shown to all men by the masters of the search and throughout all time. So now let us look, just look at one of Wittgenstein's examples. Writing about how our words are entangled in false assumptions about what we know about ourselves, he asks:

Are the words "I am afraid" a description of a state of mind?

I say "I am afraid"; someone else asks me: "What was that? A cry of fear; or do you want to tell me how you feel; or is it a reflection of your present state?"—Could I always give him a clear answer? Could I ever give him one?

We can imagine all sorts of things here, for example:

"No, no! I am afraid!"

"I am afraid. I am sorry to have to confess it."

"I am still a bit afraid, but no longer as much as before."

"At bottom, I am still afraid, though I won't confess it to myself."

"I torment myself with all sorts of fears."

"Now, just when I could be fearless, I am afraid!"

To each of these sentences a special tone of voice is appropriate, and a different context.

It would be possible to imagine people who as it were thought much more definitely than we, and used different words where we use only one.

We ask "What does 'I am frightened' really mean, what am I referring to when I say it?" And of course we find no answer, or one that is inadequate. The question is: "In what sort of context does it occur?"

I can find no answer if I try to settle the question "What am I referring to?" "What am I thinking when I say it?" by repeating the expression of fear and at the same time attending to myself, as it were observing my soul out of the corner of my eye. I can indeed ask "Why did I say that, what did I mean by it?"—and I might answer the question too; but not on the ground of observing what accompanied the speaking. And my answer would supplement, para-phrase, the earlier utterance.

What is fear? What does "being afraid" mean? If I wanted to define it at a *single* showing—I should *play-act* fear.

Could I also represent hope in this way? Hardly. And what about belief?

Describing my state of mind (of fear, say) is something I do in a particular context. . . . Is it, then, not surprising that I use the same expression in different games? And sometimes as it were between games?

And do I always talk with a very definite purpose?—And is what I say meaningless because I don't?*

Thus the *Philosophical Investigations*. Wittgenstein proceeds page after page holding the mirror up to our language and gradu-ally the reader comes to realize the astonishing fact that our hu-man language is built around some assumption, some immense fact that is not really true for us. Our language seems to have been constructed—language itself seems to have been constructed—to serve another sort of being than we ourselves really are! What sort of being? What factor in human nature is human language de-signed to reflect and serve? Our ordinary language is like the tracks of some living being who is no longer there. What manner of life is that? Where has it gone?

The answer is as simple as it is shocking. As it takes form before us, something begins to remember itself in us, some inde-structible truth that sends roots down to the great ideas of Plato, Socrates, Pythagoras:

Our language is originally built around the realities of self-attention. That is, human language is meant to be the instrument

*Ibid., pp. 187–188.

of a conscious being, a being who is fully and precisely aware of all that takes place within his own psyche. Such self-attention has disappeared from our lives, but the corresponding instrument of language remains. We have no real self-attention, yet the shells of human language remain. This is the source of the confusions and ambiguities that Wittgenstein points out to us.

The scientifically precise language, the language of logical mechanisms that Wittgenstein portrayed in his earlier work, the *Tractatus,* is the language and thinking of the computer mind. Thus it seems better to us, it seems like an ideal. But in fact it is lower, far lower than the life hinted at but no longer existent in our everyday ordinary language. Man now lives between languages—drifting more and more toward the computer language of the mechanical mind, further and further away from the life of self-attention that lies hidden as a call in the forms of ordinary life, ordinary language. There is not a single contradiction pointed to by Wittgenstein in the *Investigations* that would not be resolved by men who had the power to see themselves through the faculty of real attention, real self-confrontation. All the perplexities and ambiguities pointed out by Wittgenstein vanish instantly when the state of consciousness called self-attention exists and is real. But we have no authentic self-attention, we only imagine that we do.

The work of Wittgenstein permits contemporary man to bring the ancient purpose of philosophy back into our lives. The eternally recurring problems and crises of human life express themselves in our time through the medium of science and technology. The forms these problems have taken are a direct result of the hope which modern man has naively placed in the power and goodness of science. In its beginning, when the scientific revolution began, this hope was in fact an expression of *eros*—the feeling for truth in front of the greatness and order of the universal world. But all too soon this hope shifted, subtly and invisibly, into a trust in the automatic mind. The principles of logic and the rationalistic organization of data—which originally served as instruments and tools of *eros*—became themselves the sole object of man's trust. The philosophy of Wittgenstein shows us that in putting all our trust in this aspect of science we are pinning our hopes on a very small part of the human psyche and turning away from the possible activation of an entirely different level of mind and experience. Taken as a whole, his writings show that modern man lives neither by logic nor by mind in its higher sense. We are stranded in between the automatic and the authentic and are under the illusion that believing in the former brings us closer to the latter.

Conclusion

The conclusion of this book takes place in my living room in San Francisco on a Friday evening in March of 1982. Before submitting the final version of the manuscript to the publisher, I had asked two old friends to read it over and make suggestions—one of them an old classmate of mine from college who was now a professor of philosophy at a university in Massachusetts.

The other was a businessman with an interesting background. As a young man, he had stayed in Japan after World War II and spent nine years in a Buddhist monastery—this well before Zen Buddhism was even heard of in the West. After leaving the monastery, he married and divorced a Japanese woman and then "searched" throughout the Middle East and Europe, traveling on a small inheritance. In France he converted to Catholicism. There he started an import business that made him a considerable amount of money, but in 1968, he met a Tibetan lama in Paris and followed him to California after liquidating his commercial interests. Within a year, however, he abandoned the Tibetan, settled into a good marriage, and successfully established himself as an investment broker. I met him in 1975 through purely social channels and came to value his friendship and his good sense enormously. There was something about him. He had not abandoned his spiritual search. I knew for certain that he had found some serious teaching or path that was neither conventional nor cultish, but he never spoke about it and I never questioned him about it. This trait alone made him a very rare species among Californians.

My old classmate, Seth, had come to Berkeley for the spring academic recess to visit his older daughter, who had just given birth to his first grandchild, and, of course, I invited him to my house for dinner. Joe Petrakis, my other friend, was a frequent guest in my house and so I decided to face the music with both of them together.

During the dinner Joe and Seth both remained ominously silent about my manuscript. Once or twice when Carla, my wife, brought up some serious subject that could have been construed as relating to the book, they each shied away from it. I began to imagine terrible things and started girding my mind for an on-slaught from two quite different directions—from Seth, who was a gifted and highly respected scholar, and from Joe, who had led a very varied life and who, along the way, had acquired consider-able personal experience of the realities of the inner life.

My two teenage children were also at the table—Rafe, who was home from college for the week, and my sixteen-year-old daughter, Eve. When the meal was over they excused themselves and went out together. The atmosphere suddenly became serious and we all moved quietly into the living room.

We gathered around the coffee table—Joe and Seth sitting next to each other on the couch right under our two intimidating Chinese ancestor portraits. Joe Petrakis is a heavy-set man in his fifties with close-cropped white hair, a swarthy face, and large warm dark eyes widely separated by a big fleshy nose. He looks like a huge, friendly frog and, with his raspy voice, he sounds like one, too. Seth, on the other hand, is built like a praying mantis— well over six feet tall, all arms and legs, a long narrow face, and a high forehead piled up with deep furrows. Behind thick, rimless spectacles, his brilliant eyes looked even bigger than Joe's.

I poured brandy all around, feeling like an insect about to be eaten.

"Well," I said, "what do you think?"

Seth reached into his inside pocket for several sheets of neatly folded paper upon which he had written his notes. He leaned forward to examine the notes and his eyeglasses slid down to the end of his proboscis. "There are one or two things I'm not entirely clear about, Jerry."

When a philosophy professor starts off like that it is not a good sign.

He continued. "Your main point in the first part of the book seems to be that people are unable to live their lives according to what you call 'great ideas.' You seem to be opposed to 'mere' ideas in the absence of some sort of sustained existential confrontation with oneself. At the same time, you speak of the need to penetrate behind the world of appearances and you claim that this is the aim of philosophy. I gather that this penetration behind the world of appearances is linked to the confrontation with oneself that you speak of and which is symbolized by the figure of Socrates. Then you offer a fairly destructive criticism of the history of philosophy in the West, even, it seems, including Plato. You accuse philosophers of tinkering with great ideas—what you call 'awakening' ideas—or, worse yet, of inventing ideas out of whole cloth, or unconsciously substituting what you call concepts for real ideas. The distinction between concepts and ideas, I gather, is that concepts are like instruments for the logical organization of sensory data, whereas ideas are for awakening *eros* and guiding the individual's sustained confrontation with the whole of himself. Is that correct so far?"

I nodded yes without much enthusiasm. It is never pleasant to be summarized. Seth went on.

"In the second part of the book you write about your experiences at the high school and, in this section, so far as I can see, your purposes are fourfold." Seth looked down at his notes. "First, to exemplify the experience of *eros* through a sort of quasi-novelistic portrayal of your work with the children—the children more or less symbolize *eros* in the overall structure of human nature; second, to argue indirectly for a philosophy of education that gives primary importance to the philosophical impulse in young people; third, to demonstrate in a literary fashion the existence of philosophical questions behind the collective and personal problems that beset us as a society and as individuals—these problems are what you call 'the appearances'; and, fourth, in the chapter dealing with the parents, to show how great ideas lead to the existential confrontation of *eros* and ego, which more or less represent what you refer to as the two fundamental sides of human nature. And you end this section by indicating that philosophy can go no further than to lead the individual to a preliminary experience of this confrontation, considered as an experience of authentic self-knowledge. From that point on, what you call 'Socrates' is needed—direct guidance by a wise man or a 'guide.' "

Seth paused again to see if I had any quarrel with his summary. Then he continued.

"In the third and last part of the book you begin by introducing the notion of three kinds of influences on the human mind: first, ideas and methods that operate within the framework of direct contact with a master such as Socrates; second, ideas that are given out to the world at large and which, even though they inevitably become mixed and diluted, function to orient individual human beings in the search for wisdom; and, third, influences that arise within the everyday, ordinary life of mankind that have to do either with the purely physical needs of man or with egoistic motives. You then place authentic philosophy in the second category and proceed to reverse your previous negative criticism of the history of Western philosophy. You argue for what you call the 'downstream appreciation' of the major philosophers of the West, which I took to be an attempt to show how the historically important philosophers, whether they know it or not, are channels for the dissemination of ideas which, in their pure or complete form, originated in the first category.

"At the same time, in this third part of the book, as you offer your 'downstream appreciation' of Descartes, Hume, Kant, and

Wittgenstein, you also try to relate their ideas to certain issues that modern people now face in the form of painful problems needing solutions: the ecological crisis, for example, or the general problem of advancing scientific technology, or the problem of individual self-definition, especially in front of the fact of death. The central idea for which all these modern philosophers serve as a vehicle is, in your judgment, what you call the ancient idea of the two worlds both within and outside of human nature. Sometimes you refer to these two worlds as two movements or two directions. And again, you suggest, through your commentary on these philosophers, that the experiential encounter of these two realities— as you also sometimes refer to them—produces the state of self-questioning, which state you seem to equate in some measure with *eros* itself. Your point seems to be that behind the appearances, which take the form of the fundamental social and personal problems of life, one must discern these two movements. And the discerning of these two movements is equivalent to a profound state of self-questioning. Thus you repeat the formula, 'behind the appearance lies the Question.' You imply and you also explicitly claim that through the internal encounter of these two forces a higher quality of consciousness can manifest itself within the individual. I gather that this process is what you refer to at the beginning of the book by the Platonic term 'remembering.' This higher quality of consciousness that somehow emerges in the internal encounter of the two forces is itself, or leads to, the development of a unique power of understanding which can actually begin to answer the eternal questions about reality and the meaning of life which philosophers have traditionally asked."

Seth put down his papers. I poured myself a second brandy. He crossed his skinny legs, grasped his knee with his hands, and learned forward. "Is that a fair summary?" he asked. "You are a devil," I said, nodding affirmatively.

Apparently missing the point of my little joke, he said, "There are several points I'd like to clear up before getting to the main problem I have with your argument." (Joe Petrakis snorted at the word "argument." I poured him a second brandy.) "Your use of the term *eros* doesn't seem to correspond fully to Plato's use of the term. In the *Symposium*, *eros*, as the intermediary between the gods and men, goes both ways. He not only transmits from men to the gods, but also from the gods to men. Yet you seem to limit the term to the first meaning and you almost entirely omit the second aspect. Platonic *eros* is not only man's striving for Being, but, as it were, Being reaching down to man."

"They're the same thing," said Joe suddenly. Seth turned to him and waited for him to go on. So did I. I surmised that Joe, familiar as he was with Buddhist meditation and with the practices of contemplative Christianity, was thinking of the notion that man's turning toward the higher was already the action in him of the higher. But Joe said nothing further for the moment. Seth, slightly annoyed and embarrassed, nodded and turned his attention back to me. "Well," he said, "it's only a minor scholarly point and doesn't affect the thrust of your argument.

"I have a more serious difficulty, though still only from the point of view of historical scholarship, with your reading of the modern philosophers. I can accept the use you make of Pythagoras and Socrates, and even of Plato. Pythagoras long ago slipped into the realm of legend. No one will ever know exactly who he was or what went on around him—and, actually, I suspect that he himself and his circle were involved in roughly the sort of thing you write about. He must have been a sage and spiritual guide of some kind. And I not only accept, but approve and admire what you have made of Socrates. He, too, has long been a legend and a symbol, even though scientific scholarship still has hopes of inferring the literal facts about him. There's no figure quite like Socrates in our civilization—both wholly historical and unspokenly symbolical. In this, he's come out in better shape, as I see it, than Jesus Christ. What you've made of Socrates is excellent—a metaphor of the immense power of self-inquiry. As for Plato, well, I gnashed my teeth in places, but no one can own Plato either.

"It's much harder for me to accept the way you've handled the modern philosophers. What exactly do you mean that they were channels of esoteric ideas? What you call 'downstream appreciation'—is that anything more than a euphemism for Jacob Needleman's personal interpretations? Take your treatment of Kant, for instance—"

But at that moment, Joe, who had been growing increasingly restless, and who had already downed his third brandy, interrupted the flow of Seth's critique.

"That is all beside the point," he rumbled. "The point is that you can't live a real life simply by rubbing ideas together. People want to live. They want to know how to live. They want to know why their lives are a mess and how to change their lives. Philosophy is just philosophy; it's just talk. People talk and talk. And some people talk on paper and give it the grandiose name of philosophy. If you ask me, philosophy is just the history of talking. Philosophers would rather talk than live."

Joe turned from Seth to me. No matter how fierce he sounded, his eyes always seemed to dance.

"As books go," he said, "your book is not too bad. But all those things you write about—confronting oneself, bridging the two natures of man, experiencing the wish for truth no matter where it leads—are fantastically difficult to experience in reality." Joe poured himself another drink. "Jesus Christ died on the cross; Gautama Buddha wandered and starved in the forests of India for that sort of thing. Why do you insist on writing about it? Do you think what anyone says will bring someone else a single step closer to it?"

After a slight pause that was strangely easy and comfortable, Seth said, "Do you mind if I finish what I was saying?"

"Go right ahead," said Joe with an amiable grunt.

"I'll come to my main criticism and skip what I was going to say about your reading of Kant and Wittgenstein. You probably anticipated it anyway," said Seth, holding out his glass for a refill. I nodded at him and poured the brandy.

"My objection—or, rather, my question—is very simply put," he said. "What you call great ideas are clearly what you assume to be true ideas—that is, ideas that reflect what is the case in the universe. But you nowhere offer an argument for the truth of these ideas. Just because an idea evokes a deep question, that doesn't make it true. I mean, are you a philosopher or a theologian? For example, take this idea of the two worlds which is so central to the book. Why should I believe it? You even say somewhere that philosophy is the art of independent reflection about reality. So why don't you offer some independent reflection about this idea itself? Or are we to assume that Pythagoras and Plato cannot possibly err. If so, it's theology, not philosophy. Or perhaps you're only writing literature, or history of ideas, or psychology of education—in which case, I withdraw my objection but then replace it with a bigger objection: You're writing about philosophy without actually doing philosophy!"

I confess that a shudder went through me. For a moment I had the sense that everything I had written was built on sand, that I had neglected the most important point. My mind raced for ways to answer Seth and refute his objection. When I looked up at him I saw him as he appeared when we were undergraduates prowling the Harvard Square coffee shops late at night, hunched over a table at Hayes-Bickford's or Albiani's, arguing with each other about some point or other that was raised in class that day. He was even thinner as a young man, but the creases in his forehead, although just as numerous then, were not quite so deep, and would appear, as though by magic, only when he was reaching for some particularly complicated thought. They now seemed to be a permanent part of his face.

I realized that there was no way I could answer Seth. He had me. The interesting thing, however, was that it didn't matter. Was it the three brandies I had drunk? In any case, I found myself seeing Seth as though he were even younger than when I knew him in college. The words "as though" are not strong enough. I had the clear sensation of seeing him as he actually was when he was an adolescent. It was almost a hallucination. Perhaps it was triggered unconsciously by my thoughts about the book, especially the chapters dealing with my high-school students. I saw a tall, gangling adolescent, all arms and legs, with a big head and masses of hair shooting out like quills.

I began to realize what I had left out of the book, and why. Looking at the "adolescent" in front of me, I began to understand something new about the whole question of the influence of authentic philosophical ideas. But my sense of this was still extremely tentative.

I asked Joe what he thought of Seth's objection. He answered, as I expected, that the question of proof did not interest him at all. The problem was one of living, not of thinking, he said. He referred to the phrase I had made use of early in the book: "the myth of responsibility." He agreed with the diagnosis of the human condition that I had presented—that the convictions of the mind have no power over the other parts of our nature; that man is not *responsible* in that sense. He then spoke of his own personal life in a way that I had never heard him speak before. He spoke quietly this time, in a raspy near whisper:

"I lived for almost ten years in a Buddhist monastery in Japan. Within a week after I left the monastery, I became embroiled in a foolish and destructive relationship with a Japanese woman and this led to many other things even more foolish. It took me two years to extricate myself from it. I asked myself why, after ten years of meditating, I still didn't know how to live. I went from place to place trying to understand that. When I became a Catholic it was because I had more or less come to the conclusion that no human effort could bring me the freedom I was looking for. I felt that all I could do was to surrender myself to the Church. But I could not even surrender myself. I met another Buddhist teacher who seemed to understand my difficulty. He spoke of adapting the ancient tradition to the conditions of modern life. I soon discovered that, for me, it was all only an idea; the whole thing, the whole teaching—Buddhism, Christianity, and all the rest—were only ideas. That's why I just reacted in the way I did, so please forgive me if I'm impatient with talk about ideas."

When Joe finished speaking, a great calm filled the room. We all felt it—Carla, Joe, Seth, and myself. I don't know how to express what was so clear at that moment. There was truth in the room and everyone sensed it. How did it happen? On the one hand, truth could not be proved. On the other hand, truth could not be lived. Yet there it was, surrounding us. I saw in myself—and I think each of us experienced this in our own way—that there was now a certain balance and equilibrium. It confirmed what I had begun to suspect after Seth had finished speaking. There is such a thing as higher influences. But the way they act upon us is always new and unanticipated, and they always require something new and unanticipated in ourselves—namely, need. To act on us, truth requires *eros*.

I began to revise in my mind all the formulations I had come to about great ideas and the awakening of *eros*, the need for being. Throughout this book, I have spoken of the role of authentic philosophy as the awakener of *eros*. Now I see that this way of putting it is incomplete. The wish, the need, has to exist first, and only then can great ideas have power in one's life. Ideas do not awaken *eros*. Rather, great ideas attain their action in life only because of the energy that human beings bring to them. Ideas do not have energy; people do. The heart of philosophy is in myself.

This need, I see, has a particular flavor unlike every other desire I know. It is strangely free of tension and violence. In its presence all the parts of myself which I am aware of seem to take their proper place, or move toward their proper place. The influences I have been writing about support that movement, that internal condition that Plato described as "no part of the soul doing the work of another."

I tried to open the conversation along these lines. In front of me was this extraordinary image of "Plato's Mirror": the outer society as a mirror of the "inner society"—the arrangement of parts within the social world as a mirror or result of the arrangement of parts in the inner world. Without internal "morality" there can be no external morality. Crime in all its forms occurs out there only because the same crime is occurring within ourselves.

If there is hatred, violence, and disorder among human beings, it is because there is violence and disorder among the parts of myself: thought inflicting its formulas upon the body, which has its own kind of mind; instinctual and sexual energy in turn fueling the impulses of the mental personality—breeding fear, possessiveness, aggression, cruelty; the energy of feeling blindly merging with ideals and intentions formed out of prejudice and the naive reflexes of physical survival—loyalties to family, tribe, nation, race, social class. This whole state of affairs in which one part of the self usurps, steals from the other parts, is covered over by theories, concepts, illusions—while inside the organism, the situation is maintained by conditioned habits of self-justification and physical tension. The name for this entire state of affairs? *Egoism.*

Modern psychology began its mission in the world with a glimpse of this situation, a theoretical understanding that the world is what it is because man is what he is internally. However, it had no authentic philosophy to guide it, no understanding of the real nature of the ruling principle that can appear within the human organism. Therefore it could never succeed in bringing inner order into the life of man. Psychology does not see the ruling principle. It rejects the vision of traditional religion which holds that the ruling principle exists within the human mind and heart under the names of soul, free will, the rational mind.

In this conflict between modern psychology on the one hand and conventional religion on the other—both sides are wrong and both sides are right. Religion is right to speak of a higher principle of consciousness within the mind, but wrong to assume that it actually functions. Psychology is right to deny that there is such a principle operating in the mind, but wrong to proceed blindly ignoring its existence as a possibility to be developed. It is there, but it is asleep, and neither modern religion nor modern science has understood this.

This principle awakens in the moment of the desire for truth, the moment of *eros*. When this need is activated, I observe that in myself something quite still appears and is obeyed by other parts of my inner nature that ordinarily go their own way, taking the rest of me with them, each in their turn. In the ordinary life of people, no one, man or child, is closer to the possession of moral power than when he is in the state of wonder or in any of the other states related to it.

This need for truth is the embryo of the ruling principle. It is delicate, fragile, weak, shy, easily covered over. It is not yet the inner master spoken of in the ancient teachings. It is quite far from that immense force. But it is the beginning of it. When it is activated, "inner morality" is, for a moment, a fact.

Higher influences—such as authentic philosophy, myth, religious ideals, certain kinds of art, ritual, and custom handed down from ancient times—act upon man to support the condition of "inner morality" in which the parts of human nature do not seek gain from the other parts, but these influences cannot create this internal state of affairs directly. The direct cause is itself internal. The direct cause is the desire for truth and being. These higher influences speak directly to this special impulse in man and support it. If that impulse is not there, or is too deeply buried under egoistic habits and thoughts, then these influences cannot and do not act at all.

In our era, religious ideals seem utterly unable to act in this way for most of us. The cause of this lies in what modern man has made of religion generally. The ancient myths also have been denatured due to the influence of the scientific canons of knowledge. Ancient rituals and customs have almost all been lost or altered so that nothing of their action remains in the life of contemporary man. As for art, we are waiting for those artists to appear who can channel this sort of influence in their prod⌐ctions; in the meantime, the influence of the sacred art of the past and the metaphysically searching art of the modern era has been neutralized by museum and academic mentalities, and by the motives of financial profit and investment.

This book, then, is a plea for the return of one of the modalities of this higher influence in human life—philosophy, philosophical ideas.

The proper response to Joe Petrakis's objection that ideas by themselves have no power to change the ontological quality of human life—ideas by themselves do not raise an individual's level of being—was now clearer to me. He was right, of course; ideas alone change nothing essential in man. Yet the wish for truth does change us, if only for an instant. This sacred impulse in man is actually an energy moving within the human organism but it needs to be sought for, recognized, and, when it appears, supported in the correct way. For many of us, access to it begins in the intellect, with the intellectual interest in authentic philosophical questions as they emerge within the rough and tumble of everyday life. One sees that there are ideas that strengthen the action of this need for truth both at the merely intellectual level and, to a certain extent, deeper down at the organic level as well.

Simply introducing moral imperatives or metaphysical doctrines into human life will do nothing of itself. They have to be articulated, redefined, and given out in a manner that actually responds to the wish for truth, the only really nonegoistic impulse accessible to most modern people. Without the experience of internal morality, the ideal of external love and morality remains only a mirage. And it is from behind this mirage that the terrifying manifestations of the human unconscious appear both in the collective life of man and in our individual lives. It is from behind this mirage of responsibility that war and violence and all forms of brutality and injustice appear.

This mirage—this myth of responsibility—is constantly forming in the history of human society and in the life of the individual. Ideas and teachings that once had the effect of supporting *eros*—and the harmonizing action of *eros* upon the psychophysical structure of man—inevitably become mixed with egoistic influences and begin to act in quite the opposite way. That is, ideas become mere concepts and are mixed with mere concepts. Ideals of moral behavior and altruism, for example, which speak of sacrificing personal gain for the welfare of others, inevitably are altered in such a way that their internal psychological effect is the opposite of their external content. They speak of harmony, balance, sacrifice to the good of the whole, yet their internal action upon the mind is to breed agitation in its many forms—self-righteousness, paranoia, fear, impatience, anger, violence—all of which are signs that internally one part of the human structure is appropriating energies meant for another part. This is especially true of the action of sexual energy within human nature—as Freud in his fashion saw, and, of course, as was taught by Plato in the *Republic*. The myth of responsibility forms when outer morality is urged upon men through methods that produce and sustain inner immorality, inner imbalance, disequilibrium—"one part of the soul doing the work of another." It is therefore no wonder that man cannot live according to the ideas he holds to be true. Our ideals of morality have an "immoral" action upon us. *The struggle to be what we know is already lost in the unbalanced manner in which this knowledge enters us.*

Ideas cannot create the internal wish for truth in man, but they can attract and support that wish, that special quality of attention that Plato designated by the term *eros*. If an individual observes himself in the moments when that attention is active within him, he will see that *for that brief space of time he is actually a moral being*. No man can commit a crime in the state of wonder, or in the state of authentic remorse, or in the moment of organic grief, or in any of the fleeting states of presence in which the ruling energy of truth makes contact with the ordinary functions of the human organism.

To bring man to this perception is the ultimate purpose of authentic philosophy. Its influence can go no further. Beyond this threshold lies the work of consciously strengthening the power of my attention to truth which, in its mature form, is the only power in man worthy of the ancient name of *Mind*. Only such a work can transform man from a confused animal troubled by fleeting glimpses of moral power into . . . into what?

Enter Socrates.

A Note About the Author

Jacob Needleman is professor of philosophy at San Francisco State University. He was educated in philosophy at Harvard, Yale, and the University of Freiburg and received training in clinical psychology at the West Haven, Connecticut, Veterans Administration Hospital. He has also served as research associate at the Rockefeller Institute for Medical Research and was a research fellow at Union Theological Seminary. He is the author of *The New Religion*, *A Sense of the Cosmos*, *Lost Christianity*, and *The Way of the Physician* and was general editor of the Penguin Metaphysical Library. In addition to his teaching and writing, he serves as consultant in the fields of education, medicine, and philanthropy.